Sermons I Love to Preach

Books by the same author

◆

THE ROYALTY OF THE PULPIT,

LORDS OF SPEECH,

A MAN STOOD UP TO PREACH,

ETC.

SERMONS
I LOVE
TO
PREACH

EDGAR DeWITT JONES

Harper & Brothers, Publishers
New York

Library of Congress catalog card number: 53-5441

*To the Majestic Fraternity of the High
Calling Irrespective of Denominational
Lines This Book Is Gratefully Inscribed*

Acknowledgments

To "Hilda," Mrs. William Clark, my efficient and patient secretary, in the typing of her fourth book for me. And likewise to "Sir William," her husband, who is a book lover and an able critic.

To the Christian Board of Publication, St. Louis, for permission to use "The Greatening of Abraham Lincoln," prize-winning sermon.

To the W. B. Conkey Company, Chicago, for permission to use the lines by Ella Wheeler Wilcox.

To Dodd, Mead & Company, New York, for the privilege of quoting "Death Is a Door," by Nancy Byrd Turner.

To the Abingdon-Cokesbury Press, Nashville, for permission to include in this volume my sermon "If I Sat Where They Sit."

To Thomas Curtis Clark, for the privilege of using his fine poem on Abraham Lincoln, "The Victim," and three lines from "God's Dreams."

To Therese Lindsey for permission to quote the lines from her poem, "The Man Christ."

To the Macmillan Company for permission to quote eight lines from Vachel Lindsay's "Abraham Lincoln Walks at Midnight in Springfield, Illinois."

To Dr. Mary Brent Whiteside for her kindness in allowing me to use four lines from her poem, "Who Has Known Heights."

And to the publishers of *Lyrics of Lowly Life,* for the courtesy of quoting a stanza from Paul Laurence Dunbar's "Ere Sleep Come Down to Soothe the Weary Eyes."

To scores of my preacher friends—a gallant company—whose friendship I prize and whose letters and personal words of appreciation I cherish, now and always.

To an unnamed host who heard me preach these sermons and went out of their way to let me know how much they were helped thereby along life's pilgrimage. With St. Paul, I say of these: "I thank my God upon all my remembrance of you."   E. DeW. J.

Contents

Contents

By Way of Preface

In Which I Share Some of My
Sermonic Secrets with the Reader

THE publishers have requested me "to share with your friends the homiletical principles which have guided you in the preparation and delivery of sermons." I cheerfully comply with this request, for who can say "No" to the man who prints and circulates your books? Moreover, since this is my tenth sermonic volume, and perchance my last, I welcome the opportunity to trace my experiences in making, remaking and delivering what the late Professor William Cleaver Wilkinson aptly called "pulpit discourse." But a far better reason for acceding to the request of the publishers is the fact that I am keenly aware of the eagerness of ministers generally to learn how their comrades of the High Calling prepare and preach their sermons.

As a long-time collector of autobiographies of preachers, I have been disappointed in the failure of the authors to tell their readers how they go about this great business of preaching. The only inexhaustible mine of information on this engaging subject with which I am familiar, is the famous seriate known as *The Lyman Beecher Lectureship on Preaching*, founded at Yale University in 1871, and still strong and vibrant. In this series, among others are such giants of the pulpit as Robert W. Dale, Phillips Brooks, Charles Silvester Horne, John Henry Jowett, and, supremely, Henry Ward Beecher—who tell just about all they know on the theme, and their knowledge in that field was prodigious.

Some preacher celebrities are chary about disclosing their patterns of workmanship, while others equally famous converse freely and fascinatingly on what goes on in their workshops. Phillips Brooks, however, was reluctant to permit his friends to meddle with his manuscripts. Dr. Allen, in his massive biography of the great Bostonian, quotes the following incident:

His reticence about his method of work is shown by this anecdote. A clerical friend entering his study took up from the table the plan of a sermon just finished. "Oh, is this the way you do it?" "Put that paper down," said Mr. Brooks sternly. "No, I've got the chance and I am going to know how it's done." *"Put that paper down or leave the room."*

This seems severe and unlike the noble Bishop, but it is just possible that his visitor was "nosy" and merited the rebuke.

And now, here I am unbosoming myself homiletically, with my literary garments laid at the feet of the publisher, who is not only consenting to the act, but alas! is also abetting it. Very well, so mote it be!

I

At the close of my seminary year in 1900, I took residence in the then little town of Erlanger, Kentucky, some seven miles from Cincinnati, Ohio, and on the Southern Railroad. Three months earlier I had become the student preacher of four churches in near-by Boone County, three in small villages and one wholly rural. I preached two sermons in each of these four churches once a month. One of my charges was at Bullittsville, which supplied the locale for a book entitled *Fairhope, the Annals of a Country Church*, which was brought out by the Macmillan Company in 1917.

One reason I chose Erlanger as my residence was because of its proximity to a large city, and I took advantage of the nearness to Cincinnati by hearing eminent speakers, haunting bookshops and widening my acquaintance among the leaders of my communion, the headquarters of which was then in that city. Those were horse-and-buggy days, but automobiles were beginning to appear on the turnpikes. I reached my appointments by livery rigs, and rarely spent more than a day or two in the community —that is, not until I met a certain fair Kentucky lady in one of my churches—but that is another story!

I linger on these years in northern Kentucky because they relate intimately to the formation of study habits which definitely shaped my preparation for pulpit responsibilities. I had no pastoral burdens to speak of; my chief duties were to prepare and preach two sermons on Sunday in the churches I served. Thus it was my good fortune to have all the time I needed for sermon making, reading and writing. Few young ministers have been so privileged in this respect as was I, half a century ago.

Until the time of my marriage in 1902, to the fair lady already alluded to, I boarded at a farmhouse on the edge of town. Five years after we had left Erlanger, we enjoyed a visit with the hospitable family with whom for a year or more I had made my home. On this occasion my farmer host took me out to show me the path I had worn along the edge of a field as I went over my sermons. That trail was still easy to trace.

I wrote out in full both morning and evening sermons in my Erlanger days, frequently making as many as three drafts before I was satisfied with what I had written. By then the sermon was deep in my subconscious mind and was part of me, nor did I consciously memorize the manuscript. I made outlines of the sermons but did not take so much as a single note into the pulpit, a practice I have continued through all the years of my ministry.

It was in those years that I cultivated what I call the brooding habit; that is, I brooded over texts, Scriptural passages and subjects upon which I planned to preach. I have long cherished quiet, uninterrupted hours for this brooding process, and somehow have managed to keep my preparation periods inviolate, even during the ministry of large city churches. In 1902 I organized a church of the Disciples of Christ in Erlanger, with forty-seven members, composed mostly of families who were employed in Cincinnati or Covington, and had built or bought homes in that fast-growing town. I then divided my time between Bullittsville and Erlanger and led a church-building project in the latter place, procuring much of the fund, and likewise three spacious and beautiful memorial windows. About this time I began to write articles for the religious press and to appear on programs at county and district conventions, my usual assignment—a sermon.

I think I am factual in saying that during the three years in northern Kentucky I laid the foundation for my study habits and sermon construction. Perhaps this fact, coupled with a facility for public speech and boundless enthusiasm, had something to do with my being called from Erlanger to the ministry of one of our old and thriving congregations, the Franklin Circle Christian Church, Cleveland, Ohio.

Looking back on that event, I marvel at my courage—or was it just sheer foolhardiness? I am not sure. The thoughts of young preachers are long, long thoughts, and the Lord must have had a hand in it, for Franklin Circle years were years of discipline and beautiful friendships. Returning there on November 10, 1952, to speak at the one hundred and tenth anniversary of this good church, I felt the peace of great memories.

II

The preparation of sermons fit to preach is, I hold, an "ordeal." The dictionaries define the word as "any severe trial or experience." Preparing to preach is a heavy trial and a grinding pursuit. But no more so than writing books, painting pictures, mastering a musical instrument, or managing a business. There is no short cut to any career worth claiming. To be sure, the good workman in any realm gathers momentum as he goes and does his task more expertly. Yet an ordeal it is, and one comes to love it, too. Did not a famous painter when asked to explain how he achieved such exquisite colors reply, "I mix my colors with my lifeblood"? Good preaching, as my friend and mentor, the late Dr. George Hamilton Combs, used to say, "is bloodletting."

Into the ordeal of sermonic preparation must go wide and selective reading, together with much exacting writing. All my life I have loved books. I began as a boy to build up a library, and I still add to my collection, which now numbers above six thousand volumes. I early specialized in biography, history, homiletics and poetry. I can say also that my theological shelves are not only respectable but the volumes are down to date. My debt to biography is unpayably great, and the autobiographies of noted preachers fascinate me as do few other books. Sometimes I think I read too much, for I am always reading, in sleeping-car berths, in hotel rooms, and continually in my home library.

Francis Bacon says that "reading makes a full man, conference a ready man, and writing an exact man. . . . Histories make men wise; poets, witty; the mathematics, subtle; natural philosophy, deep; moral, grave; logic and rhetoric, able to contend." And he goes on to say that "manners are influenced by studies." All of these qualities are involved in the preparation of sermons, although mathematics in my case have been the least helpful. In this I have something in common with Henry Ward Beecher, who didn't do well with that subject in college, or anywhere else. If there is a substitute for mathematics as a disciplinary measure, I should suppose it to be the languages, and, especially, Latin and Greek.

Usually I began my preparation of the sermon on Monday, selecting the subject which seemed at the time to be most preachable and over which I had brooded in off hours. Sometimes the choice was easy, because of my mood or due to events in the life of the congregation, community, or nation. Once the decision was made, I would draw up a rough draft; then followed this with a more carefully composed manuscript of, say, six or seven hundred words. With this I toyed, making slight changes, and trying to find the right word at the right place. Next, I called in my secretary, who typed as I dictated. Four secretaries out of the five I had during the major part of my ministry became expert in typing directly from dictation.

As I dictated, I paced the floor of the study, amplifying, correcting and rectifying the sheets I held in my hand. The result would run to some fifteen hundred words, and this draft I took home and subjected to further criticism and change, with still further elaboration. I changed and bettered sentences, favoring both the short and the long, but not the too long. Having given the sheets my best thought and brought the manuscript to what I felt was completion, I turned it over to the stenographer for the final copy, which usually ran to ten pages, or above three thousand words.

It would be Friday by then, and I must get the sermon well in hand. Saturday I took it more calmly, the hard work was done. But I kept a carbon copy of the manuscript with me, even when making emergency calls, glancing over it as I rode in a taxi or was being driven to my destination by some member of the family. Saturday night, if I was not engaged, and I made an honest effort to keep Saturday nights free, I took a long walk, if the weather permitted, thinking through the sermon, but with no manuscript at hand.

Sunday morning I arose ahead of the family and brooded over the order of the morning worship; this, with a program of the service before me. Then for the final time before preaching, I read the sermon through slowly, checking to see if I had used any words of whose pronunciation I was not certain. If I found any such words, and I often did, I looked them up in my desk dictionary. Then a quiet period of preparing myself to preach and lead the congregation in prayer; a light breakfast, and I was off to the church. The time of delivery had come. If I was in my usual good health, and had a sermon in my soul, I was ready, God helping me, for the High Adventure of Preaching.

Through the twenty-six years of my Detroit ministry I followed rather closely the routine of sermon preparation as described above. Pastoral duties and exigencies of one kind or another broke in on this procedure, but nevertheless I usually managed to know where I was going when I stood up to preach. Today, as minister emeritus, when I return to preach from my old pulpit I invariably prepare a new sermon for the occasion. This is good discipline for me and good also for the congregation. Preparation of sermons is, I repeat, an ordeal, but withal a glorious one.

III

There is a hazard in the delivery of a sermon, no matter how thorough and painstaking the preparation. Something may occur to mar the conditions favorable to the effective delivery of the discourse, unexpected news of a disturbing nature which comes to the minister just before the service of worship starts; a sudden or tragic death in a family of the church; an apathetic congregation; a furious storm; a deep snow—any untoward circumstance that may deplete attendance, may throw the preacher off balance. However, nothing can so fortify the preacher against failure in any instance as careful preparation and the sensing of an invisible spiritual dynamo.

No matter how excellent the sermon, if the congregation has difficulty in hearing the speaker, the consequences are lamentable. Personally, I have never known this handicap. For ten years, I preached in Central Woodward Christian Church, Detroit, a Gothic edifice with a high vaulted ceiling, without a public-address system, and had no difficulty in making myself heard. This church has a seating capacity of 1,050, including three balconies, but not the side chapel, which can seat 124 additional worshipers. I do not think I have a remarkable voice, but it carries well. I employ a full tone, varying the pitch from time to time.

So-called big voices do not always succeed in being distinctly heard. Clear enunciation is of primary importance, and deliberate speech is more readily heard than rapid public speaking. There are exceptions to this rule. Phillips Brooks poured forth

his words at a torrential pace and was heard, but his hearers had
no time for woolgathering. My own style of speech is deliberate,
with an occasional faster tempo. The mechanics of public speech
are simple: throw the voice out, speak to the people, enunciate
distinctly, and do not drop the voice at the end of a sentence.

The most skillful of speakers will occasionally fumble a sentence, juggle a quotation, or mispronounce a word. Usually it is
not best to attempt a correction, for in so doing the attention of
the hearers is directed to a slip they probably had not noticed.
It all depends on the seriousness of the mistake, whether it
should be corrected or not.

William Jennings Bryan, whose friendship I cherished, once
told me this anecdote. A lawyer and a minister were talking
shop, and the preacher asked the lawyer what he did when he
made an error in addressing a jury, did he correct it or let it pass?
The lawyer replied that it depended on how important the error
was. If serious, he corrected it, if trivial, he let it pass. The
lawyer then asked the preacher what course he followed if he
made a mistake in the delivery of a sermon. The minister replied: "I follow your plan; if the mistake is serious I correct it,
but if it is otherwise I pay no attention to it. For instance, last
Sunday morning in my sermon I meant to say that the devil is
the father of all liars, but in the heat of delivery I said that lawyers are the fathers of liars. But it was such a small matter and
I let it pass." The story is probably apocryphal, but it is a good
story nevertheless. A little nonsense now and then is relished by
the best of preachers, for so it was with Beecher, Spurgeon, Merton S. Rice, and others of a glorious company.

I have found no small satisfaction in the ability to preach
without notes before me, but this may not be the best method
for all who preach the Word. It is not the method of many able
preachers of our day who habitually take the outline of the
sermon into the pulpit, even though they may not so much as
glance at it. The outline is there if they need it, and the best of
memories sometimes plays curious tricks. Some ministers have

photographic memories and can see clearly the outline they have made in their "mind's eye."

I am acquainted with preachers of power who seldom write their sermons in full. These men read widely, concentrate deeply, take a few notes into the pulpit, and preach acceptably, often brilliantly. A prime requisite for this pattern of preparation and delivery is an opulent vocabulary, and this the late Dr. George Hamilton Combs of Kansas City, "the nightingale of the Disciples," had. It is also true of my brilliant successor at Central Woodward Church, Dr. Perry Epler Gresham, and of other contemporaries whose sermons shine like stars in the firmament of great preaching.

Occasionally, nowadays, I preach a sermon without writing it out in full, my dependable practice. But I don't think I could do this successfully had it not been for my long discipline of *writing, writing, writing*.

Usually I preach from twenty-five to thirty minutes, occasionally, forty, but I think my average would be half an hour. Once, in Detroit, I preached an hour and five minutes, and I announced the length of the sermon the Sunday before I preached it, and so publicized it in the newspapers. My subject was "The Sixty-six Books of the Bible." I gave a lot of thought to that sermon, but I didn't write it out. The remarkable thing about this sermon was that the announcement that I was to preach an hour didn't lessen my hearing, but greatened it that Sunday.

IV

I have been called a "Biblical Preacher," and I trust I deserve the compliment. Much as I love books in general, and some books in particular, I regard the Bible as the preacher's chief textbook. Of that precious literature he ought to be a specialist, and, indeed, according to his ability, an expert. The ambition to be "mighty in the Scripture" is one of which no minister of the Word should be apologetic.

I have given many series of sermons on such themes as "The Great Books of the Bible," "The Great Chapters of the Bible," "The Great Verses of the Bible," and "The Great Doctrines of the Bible." I have bought and read scores of books about the Bible, written by qualified scholars. Commentaries, old and new, together with exegetical works have been my bread and meat. The various versions and translations of the Holy Scriptures I have found good and exciting reading.

At one time during my fourteen years pastorate in Bloomington, Illinois, I held a month of evangelistic services, preaching twenty-seven sermons from the book of Acts, beginning at chapter one and closing with the twenty-eighth. In order to familiarize the people with this thrilling section of the New Testament, I purchased three hundred copies of Acts, printed separately and bound inexpensively. These I circulated among the congregation. We had a successful meeting, with some seventy accessions to the church, and I had the time of my sermonic life! Two years later I followed the same pattern with the Gospel of Mark, which I found not quite so adaptable to such a use, but nevertheless we had a season of rejoicing; and some fifty came into the church of our Lord.

One never runs out of Biblical themes. It is a mine richer than Golconda. Spurgeon used to say that if a preacher was obliged to preach only from the eighth of Romans, he would be kept busy for the rest of his preaching days. Exceptionally busy, I would add.

V

Of the need for careful phrasing of sermon titles and for the wise choice of illustrative material I have not been unmindful. Perhaps next in importance to naming a baby is the naming of a book, a play, a song or a sermon. Some sermons name themselves; others yield stubbornly to suitable titles. Some years ago, in reviewing one of my sermonic volumes, the reviewer said that "the author had a flair for giving significant names to his brain children." I am not so sure as to that, since I can recall times when a fairly accurate description of me would have been something like this: "Wild man in search of a title!" Usually I have found what I was looking for, but not without travail and vexation of spirit.

Perhaps I should be more specific. For instance, "Blundering into Paradise," was a natural for a sermon on Luke 23:43, "And Jesus said unto him, Verily I say unto thee, Today shalt thou be with me in paradise." Likewise, although not quite so easily captured, was this title, "The Discipline of Delayed Revelations" for a sermon based on John 16:12, "I have yet many things to say unto you, but ye cannot bear them now." But a sermon contrasting Mary's gift of precious ointment given to Him while He was alive, with Joseph's gift of a tomb for His dead body, gave me trouble, and I was a long time in coming up with "Roses of Bethany and Lilies of Arimathea." My sermon on the Prodigal Son, under the caption "The Romance of God's Grace," was simply an adaptation of an old and radiant phrase. Then, "Praiseworthy Prodigality" was the name I gave a sermon from Ecclesiastes 11:1, "Cast thy bread upon the waters: for thou shalt find it after many days." One of my latest sermons is entitled "A Beautiful Blunder," and deals with Simon Peter's floundering speech on the Mount of Transfiguration.

It has been said that a sermon without illustrations is like a house without windows. The statement is apt but not wholly true. Some of the world's famous sermons are without a single illustration. However, this is exceptional, and especially so in modern preaching. On the other hand, I have known at least one famous preacher who used anecdotes lavishly and with extraordinary effect. I am referring to my long-time colleague on Woodward Avenue, Detroit, the late Dr. Merton S. Rice; yet his sermons were not merely a chain of stories told with artistry and dramatic action. Adroitly and powerfully he wove around the anecdotes a texture of strong evangelistic preaching which made converts to the cause.

Where do I get my illustrative material? Everywhere, except in books of illustrations. I find illustrations in biography, in history, in fiction, in scientific works, in newspapers, in magazines, in the radio, in God's great out-of-doors, on street cars, in trains, in hotels, offices, shops, stores, schoolrooms, college campuses, baseball parks and churches; and also from men, women, little children, babies and the Bible. Why, "Earth's crammed with heaven, and every common bush afire with God."

That there is an element of enticement in certain types of illustrations for pulpit use almost every minister knows, or ought to know. It might be well for our preacher clan to take to heart Proverbs 1:10, "My son, if sinners entice thee, consent thou not."

Even so, unlike sermon titles, which seem to say coquettishly: "Come and catch us, if you can," illustrations have a way of shouting lustily: "Here we are, at the door; let us in and be quick about it." But there are some anecdotes that do not deserve to be let in. The stale and hackneyed, for example; and also the crude, the crass, and the story which, however clever, takes a sly dig at racial, creedal or regional idiosyncrasies. The shorter an illustration, the better, as a rule. Long stories in a sermon are hard to handle and tend to deflect auditors from the main stream of thought, but, occasionally, and particularly at the sermon's end, an incident of some length may prove climactic.

Incidents which emerge from the preacher's own experiences, if used with discrimination and not too often, can be exceptionally effective. How well I know this to be true through the popularity of three such intimate stories I have employed with impressive results: (1) The account of a visit to Trinity Church, Boston, on a bleak November weekday, and what happened there. (2) The story of my friend, a Negro headwaiter of Bloomington, Illinois, his little girl Nellie, and Madame Sarah Bernhardt receiving the family in her private car. And (3) The pathetic and tragic tale of my Dalmatian dog Prince, and the theology therein involved. All three incidents appear in sermons in this volume.

VI

It is all to the good for a dominie to have a hobby or two. Special interests of this sort keep his mind fresh and his spirits buoyant. Then, too, such a pursuit makes him more companionable, assuming he never becomes boresome in expatiating upon his favorite topic. I have three hobbies, to wit: biography, birds and Abraham Lincoln.

These lines are written in my Lincoln Room, where one wall is shelved high with nearly one thousand Lincoln books, and gazing upon me from the walls are twenty-three pictures of the uncommon commoner. A copy of Vachel Lindsay's "Abraham Lincoln Walks at Midnight in Springfield, Illinois," done for me in Vachel's unique script, is among my treasures, and I can see it as I write. I have given more speeches on Lincoln than I care to enumerate here, written three books on the absorbing theme, several monographs, and scores of newspaper and magazine articles. If I were to frame a motto for this room, it would be

LET NOT THE LINCOLN IN YOU DIE.

As for birds, I was tutored in ornithology by a friendly expert; and, dear reader, give me a day in the woods and meadows at the migration season, armed only with field glasses and Reed's *Pocket Bird Guide,* and I will, as Emerson says, make the pomp of an emperor ridiculous.

It was a day long to remember when I first glimpsed a regal pair of pileated woodpeckers at Lake Pokegma, Minnesota. Another such day was when I watched a magnificent specimen of the bald eagle soar majestically over the shores of a bay in Florida. Long ago I lost the lust to kill wild creatures, whether of land, water, or air, cherishing, as I do, a reverence for all life.

VII

As for the sermons which follow, ten are the products of my emeritus years, which began January 1, 1947. The fourth and last sermons are of the vintage of 1952. It may interest my preacher friends to learn that "Magnificent Obsession" (Chapter Thirteen), is the only sermon of my Kentucky apprenticeship that has lasted through all the intervening years. I have preached this sermon at least a hundred times, in many states, and in city and small-town churches. True, I have made some changes, and occasionally added fresh illustrations, but in the main the sermon is as when I "toiled terribly" over it, making, as I recall, four drafts before I felt it was as good as I could construct it. Long ago I lost the manuscript, and am recalling it here from memory. If awakened at midnight and asked to preach on "A Magnificent Obsession," which, by the way, was not my first title, I am sure I could comply immediately with the request. I may add that this sermon has never been in print until now.

"Jewels from King Solomon's Mines" (Chapter Twelve), I call my "hardy perennial," so often and so long have I done business with it. I estimate I have given this speech over three hundred times, as sermon, lecture, commencement or baccalaureate theme. It is one of those popular addresses which grow with the years and yet retain a modicum of freshness. It is like a train of freight cars of varying length, with the caboose ready to be attached whenever needed.

During these latter years, appearing frequently, as I do, in preaching missions, Lenten series, retreats and assemblies, I dearly love to preach "The Matterhorn of the Holy Scriptures," "If I Sat Where They Sit," "On Finding and Losing God," and "The Most Unforgettable Person I Know."

I love the ministry with a very great love. To me it has been not only an exacting but also an absorbing and exciting calling. I have not known as much as a faint shadow of regret in leaving the law office, with probably a political career in the offing, for the ministry of Jesus Christ. If I had to do it over again, I would do what I have done, only better, I trust. I pray now that I may be privileged to go on preaching, lecturing, writing, and talking books and shop with congenial friends until the bell tolls for me the last time. And, until then, I feel like saying with Van Wyck Brooks, whose books so many of us love:

> Every day
> > I begin my work with the same
> > old feeling that I am on trial for
> > my life and will probably not be
> > acquitted.

EDGAR DEWITT JONES

November, 1952

Note: Readers of published sermons should know that, with the exception of those delivered from manuscript, or stenographically reported, sermons are seldom preached precisely as printed. In process of delivery, the speaker is likely to expand, elaborate, and occasionally introduce new and pertinent material, inspired by the audience or surroundings, or both. The sermons in this volume, except chapters eleven and twelve, were expanded about a fourth in delivery.

1

The Matterhorn of the Holy Scriptures

I will lift up mine eyes unto the mountains:
From whence shall my help come?
My help cometh from the Lord,
Who made heaven and earth.
PSALM 121:1, 2 (ASV)

ONE of the most famous and majestic mountains of the world is the Matterhorn, a monarch of the Alps, 14,782 feet in height. Based on the border between Switzerland and Italy, the Matterhorn from the Swiss side looms up as an isolated obelisk. Viewed from Italian territory the Matterhorn resembles a massive, impregnable fortress shouldering out against the sky.

The ascent of this noted mountain from the Swiss side, while difficult, is readily achieved by experienced climbers. It is otherwise with the Italian side, which is a terraced wall and extremely hazardous. Not until July 14, 1865, was the summit gained from the Italian side, and three members of the party, including a guide, lost their lives as they descended the dangerous walls, where a misstep meant almost certain death.

The Matterhorn is not as high as other peaks in the vicinity, but there is a singular grandeur about it, a kind of dramatic individuality which sets it apart. Storms swirl about its rugged body and granite head. It rises majestically from its sunless pillars like a sentinel of the Most High. When the morning sun gilds its summit or the rays of the sunset paint it crimson, the beauty of the Matterhorn is indescribable.

I

What would you say is the Matterhorn of the Holy Scriptures? What mountain of Holy Writ resembles the Matterhorn in splendor and majestic massiveness? What mountain's peak of comfort, blessing, inspiration, would you choose? Opinions naturally differ. Some would choose that precious passage in Deuteronomy, the thirty-third chapter and twenty-seventh verse, "The eternal God is thy refuge, and underneath are the everlasting arms." This was a favorite Scripture of Dr. Merton S. Rice, my long-time fellow minister on Woodward Avenue and very dear friend. He quoted this passage oftener perhaps than any other and inscribed it in many guest books and wrote it in myriad letters. Others would select that inspiring verse, Isaiah 40:31, "They that wait upon the Lord shall renew their strength; they shall mount up with wings as eagles; they shall run, and not be weary; and they shall walk, and not faint." Then there are those who would say that for them the Matterhorn of the Book is the eighth verse in the sixth chapter of Micah, called by someone "the high watermark of Old Testament Scripture": "He hath shewed thee, O man, what is good; and what doth the Lord require of thee, but to do justly, and to love mercy, and to walk humbly with thy God?"

Still others would turn to the New Testament and say, "Why look further than John 3:16: 'For God so loved the world, that he gave his only begotten Son, that whosoever believeth in him should not perish, but have everlasting life.' Surely this to multitudes is the Matterhorn of the Book." Martin Luther called this verse "Little Bibles." Thus one could go on and on. Opinions would naturally differ. My own choice is the exciting culmination of the eighth chapter of Romans: "Nay, in all these things we are more than conquerors through him that loved us. For I am persuaded, that neither death, nor life, nor angels, nor principalities, nor powers, nor things present, nor things to come, nor height, nor depth, nor any other creature, shall be

able to separate us from the love of God, which is in Christ
Jesus our Lord." Professor H. H. Farmer calls this passage "the
grandest expression of faith in all literature." It is all of that
and more.

Now, before we lift our eyes to the peak of this Matterhorn
of the Bible, let us tarry briefly in the foothills. Presently we
shall set out for the grand ascent. Here in the nestling foothills
is this affirmation: "Nay, in all these things we are more than
conquerors." What things? The writer has just listed them:
Tribulation! Anguish! Persecution! Famine! Nakedness! Peril!
Sword! What headlines! These were the "things" that were
happening daily to the little company of first-century Christians. It is factual to say that the Church was born in occupied
territory and under ruthless dictators.

"Nay, in all these things we are *more* than conquerors." How
can a person be *more* than a conqueror? Is it not enough to
conquer? No, it is not. It is not enough to be elected President
of the United States. The occupant of that high office must
then give a good account of himself in office. He must take
the long view and strive to serve all the people. He must try
to forget himself into immortality. It is not enough for a minister to preach able sermons. He must strive to embody the
teachings he proclaims in daily life. It is not enough to amass
a fortune; one must know how to share it for society's good.
Alexander the Great, Napoleon and Hitler were conquerors,
but not *more* than conquerors. It is the over-plus of life, good
measure on the side of character, integrity, justice, considerateness, gallantry and good will that count. Material gains are not
enough. They must be matched by spiritual and moral gains as
well. A man may win a war and remain a brute, achieve a fortune and lack the common decencies of mind, heart and spirit.
The Duke of Wellington was more than conqueror when, sur-
veying the battlefield after Waterloo, he observed: "Next to a
great defeat, the saddest thing in the world is a great victory."
Captain Jack Phillip of the battleship *Texas,* was more than

conqueror when in the Spanish-American War, after the victory over the enemy ships, he said, "Don't cheer, boys, the poor fellows are dying." Real men and women are more than their successes, greater than their defeats, better than their material prizes.

Gaze now upon the shining summit of this Matterhorn of the Holy Scriptures before the long, steep ascent begins:

"For I am persuaded [or I am sure] that neither death, nor life, nor angels, nor principalities, nor powers, nor things present, nor things to come, nor height, nor depth, nor any other creature shall be able to separate us from the love of God, which is in Christ Jesus our Lord."

Now here are ten events, experiences, vicissitudes, stubborn facts, which seem to separate us from what we deem good, desirable, precious. Let me list them in capital letters:

DEATH!

LIFE!

ANGELS!

PRINCIPALITIES!

POWERS!

THINGS PRESENT!

THINGS TO COME!

HEIGHT!

DEPTH!

ANY CREATURE!

Think on these stubborn obstacles as facing him who would make the exciting ascent of the Matterhorn of the Bible. They represent the ice, the snow, the crevasses, the driving storms and perpendicular walls which every Alpine climber must conquer ere he stands upon the mountaintop more than conqueror.

II

Is it not an impressive fact that the apostle heads this list of obstacles with "death" as not being able to separate us from the love of God? Why did the writer list death first? Because it is by all odds the most formidable. Death has a finality that seems invincible. "By itself death seems to be fatal. Death as a finality is the supreme sarcasm of life," says Dr. George A. Gordon. The Christian faith challenges and repudiates this bleak view. Here comes a letter bearing on the passing of a grand character, saying, "Dear John is no more." "No more?" Why, that is not the language of faith. It is the speech of unbelief. "No more?" Nay, rather, more and more of the fuller life and more of that Light which shineth more and more unto the perfect day.

Yet the prospect of death is ever before us. To all outward appearance this *is* the end. We reach out lame hands, groping for other hands we shall never clasp again in the life that now is. We cry aloud and there is no reply; only silence, deep and inexorable. But this is not the answer of the Christian faith. God does not lose us in the dust of death. Here the believing, trustful heart is more than conqueror. "Death is swallowed up in victory!"

Prior to the coming of the radio I had one record I loved to play when the lights were low and all was still in the house. It was Caruso's "O Sole Mio," and I played it again and again. How vividly I recall the last time I listened to that record. I had come home at a late hour and all was quiet in the house. A single electric bulb dimly shone in the living room as I put my favorite record on the victrola. I seated myself before the fireplace, where a few embers still glowed, and the golden voice flooded the room with its melody. Then I remembered that all that was mortal of the famous tenor rested in a tomb in Naples, and yet somewhere a voice was calling, calling, vibrantly, beautifully calling.

There in the gloaming, with that great voice calling, I mused: Can it be that the invention is greater than the inventor? Does the one persist and the other perish? Do men, women and little children die and cease to be, while *things* go on forever? The recording of the glorious voice delighted me, but it did not en-

lighten. For answer to such "obstinate questionings" I turn to
the record of St. Paul's puissant words: "For I am persuaded
[I am sure] that death shall not be able to separate us from the
love of God that is in Christ Jesus our Lord."

> Death be not proud, though some have called thee
> Mighty and dreadful, for thou art not so;
> For those whom thou think'st thou dost overthrow,
> Die not, poor Death; nor yet canst thou kill me.

Thus wrote great old Dr. John Donne, who, it would appear,
was on familiar terms with the Matterhorn of the Holy
Scriptures.

Next, the apostle lists "life," rating it second to death in the
list of mysteries that perplex and disturb human beings, flinging
up obstacles which seem hard, ominous and insuperable. For
life is never all good or all evil; never all sunshine or all shadow,
though there are times when it seems either the one or the
other. I picked up a copy of the revised edition of *Bartlett's
Familiar Quotations* and turned to the hundreds of allusions to
"Life," and here are a few of the definitions I found: "Life is a
candle," "Life is a blunder," "Life is a disease," "Life is a bub-
ble," "Life is a dance," "Life is a cheat," "Life is a dream,"
"Life is sweet," "Life is bitter," "Life is a tale told by an idiot,
signifying nothing," and so on and on. I opened a book written
by a brilliant cynic and read: "Life is the jail sentence you get
for the crime of being born."

Then I took from a shelf of reference books Cruden's *Con-
cordance of the Bible,* turned to the references to "Life," and
these caught my eye: "God breathed into his nostrils the breath
of life"; "A man's life consisteth not in the abundance of the
things which he possesseth"; Jesus said, "I am the life," and "I
came to give you life and that more abundantly"; St. Paul:
"Your life is hid with Christ in God"; John, the beloved disciple: "He that hath the Son hath life"; and from the book of
Revelation: "Let him that is athirst take the waters of life

freely"; and so on and on. Life, eternal life; life hid and life revealed with Christ in God, the eternal life of the Spirit.

Life? What is life? Someone has put it thus: "Tender Teens, Teachable Twenties, Tireless Thirties, Fiery Forties, Fervent Fifties, Silvery Sixties, Saintly Seventies, Aching Eighties." Life—whatever sorrows and disappointments it may bring and however roughly it may treat us—life's vicissitudes cannot separate us from the love of God which is in Christ Jesus, our Lord.

> Life! we've been long together
> Through pleasant and through cloudy weather;
> 'Tis hard to part when friends are dear,—
> Perhaps 'twill cost a sigh, a tear;
> Then steal away, give little warning,
> Choose thine own time;
> Say not "Good night," but in some brighter clime
> Bid me "Good morning."

"Nor angels." The word means "messenger." In this sense there may be bad angels as well as good. The reference here must be to evil messengers, double dealers, false friends mouthing slanderous tales. Such messengers may separate us from peace of mind for a while, but what a boon it is to know that messengers of evil, purveyors of lies, cannot separate us from God.

"Nor principalities, nor powers." How intimately first-century Christians knew to their sorrow the long, hard conflicts with dictators and tyrants. Thus Peter and John were haled before the Council in Jerusalem and commanded "not to speak at all nor teach in the name of Jesus." Their answer is part of the heroic history of the Church when it was young. They replied: "Whether it be right in the sight of God to hearken unto you more than unto God, judge ye, for we cannot but speak the things which we have seen and heard." The powers that were could separate these brave men from their fellow Christians, but they could not separate them from God. Martin Niemoeller was separated from his church, his family and his friends by the hateful power of a tyrannical state, but not even Hitler at the peak of his dictatorship could separate Niemoeller from the love of God. Principalities and powers threaten us today where communism is rampant, but that sinister power is helpless to separate us from the love of God, which is in Christ Jesus our Lord.

"Things present," the things that trouble and perplex us *now;* disappointment, adversity, misfortunes in home, school, shop and office—how real they are and how disturbing. Once I listened to a great old man, strongly disciplined in the school of Christ. The snows of eighty winters were on his head, and his fine old face, etched by the sculpturing years, was noble and serene. He said something like this: "I have been young and now I am old. Looking back I cannot recall since boyhood a single day when everything was as I would have liked to have had it. Sometimes it was the heartaches that are inevitable in rearing a family; sometimes it was a heavy bereavement; sometimes it was financial anxieties, sometimes the falsehoods and slander which no man in public life can hope to escape. Yet I cannot recall a single day since my maturity when God's grace was other than sufficient and I fainted not because I beheld the goodness of the Lord in the land of the living."

I remember as though it happened but yesterday a late autumn day when I shaped my course to Trinity Church in Boston, a church forever linked with the noble ministry of Phillips Brooks. I went halfway up the center aisle and knelt in prayerful meditation. I thought myself alone in the sanctuary, when suddenly I heard a woman sobbing, sobbing as though her heart was breaking. As soon as my eyes became used to the fading light, I saw on the other side of the aisle, and some five or six rows ahead of me, a woman kneeling in prayer, her face buried in her hands and her slender shoulders shaking convulsively as she sobbed. Suddenly the sobbing ceased, and the suppliant arose and came down the aisle, so close to me I could have reached out and touched her. A shaft of soft light silhouetted her head and shoulders as she passed. Lo! her head was held high, her face serene, her shoulders erect. I knew then that her knees had found those altar stairs that slope through darkness up to God. The "things present," whatever they were that bowed down that woman's troubled heart, could not separate her from the love of God and his healing ministry. "Wherefore" (O mighty "Wherefore") . . . "Wherefore, my beloved brethren, be ye stedfast, unmovable, always abounding in the work of the Lord, forasmuch as ye know that your labor is not vain in the Lord" (ASV). This Matterhorn also stands undefeated by the storms that beat against it.

"Things to come." What did St. Paul mean by these words? We may not know of a certainty, but it is pleasant to speculate. Did he have in mind the victories of the gospel in prospect, the expansion of the Christian community, the ingathering of multitudes into the Church of Christ? This is believable, for it was a theme and goal dear to his heart. Was he thinking of his friends in the various Christian groups, say, the expectation of meeting with Philemon, his family, and the church that met in his home at Colossae; or perhaps a reunion with the saints at Philippi "whose names," the apostle wrote, "are in the book of life"? This is probable. Or, could he have been thinking of the bonds, the prison cells, the rough handling by adversaries? Very likely, for these were sure to come. "Things to come!" He may well have had in mind "the last things," the New Jerusalem, the Father's House not made with hands. But whatever was to come—joy, sorrow, persecution, false brethren, shipwreck, death —he could take them in stride, for he endured as seeing Him who is invisible.

> O blindness to the future! kindly giv'n,
> That each may fill his circle mark'd by Heav'n.

"Nor height, nor depth." No height of joy, no depth of anguish, no elevation to a lofty eminence of preferment, no victory or defeat shall be able to separate us from God. Witness James A. Garfield, but two months in the Presidency, saying to his

young pastor, "Let me give you a text for next Sunday. Preach
from 'I shall be satisfied when I awake with thy likeness.'" An
assassin's bullet separated Garfield from this life and his high
office, but nothing could separate him from the love of God.

Hear the prayer of the Psalmist, "Out of the depths have I
cried unto thee, O Lord. . . . My soul waiteth for the Lord more
than they that watch for the morning." Out of the depths Job
cried, "O that I knew where I might find him," and the Lord
answered Job out of the storm. Out of the depths Jesus cried,
"My God, why hast thou forsaken me," and the empty tomb
was God's answer to His Son. Deep calleth unto deep, and no
depth is deep enough to separate us from the love of God, which
is in Jesus Christ our Lord.

"Nor any other creature." Literally nothing that may yet be
created shall be able to separate us from the love of God which
is in Christ Jesus our Lord, O sing Hallelujah forth! the Lord
God omnipotent reigneth!

III

"I will lift up mine eyes unto the mountains." In 1917 with a
congenial companion I made the ascent of Mount Mitchell, in
the mountain range northeast of Asheville, North Carolina.
This is the highest mountain east of the Rockies, being 6,711
feet in elevation. We began the climb while the day was young
and walked all day along fairly well-defined trails. Sometimes
the trail was easy, sometimes steep and toilsome. At times we
passed through tangles of rhododendron and mountain laurel
and through blazing azaleas. Overhead, white clouds, like ghost
ships, sailed the blue. At sunset we arrived at Camp Alice,
where we had supper and spent the night. We slept in a tent,
and a storm broke over us during the night. The wind tore at
the canvas, threatening to take our shelter, but it held fast. The
next morning the mountain was shrouded in a ghostly mist, and
as we took the last mile of the trail we walked through an aisle
of dripping branches, and a dense fog reminiscent of old Lon-

don Town. Reaching the top, which was clear of timber, we seemed to be on an island and all around us was a shrouded sea of mist. Then, suddenly, the miracle occurred! It was as if the hand of the Eternal had swept back a colossal curtain, raised it, and lo! for miles about and beneath: the brilliant sunshine, the verdant valley, winding streams like silver ribbons crinkling their way through the valleys, smoke curling from farmhouse chimneys, cattle and sheep browsing in fields and, far off, the outlines of other mountains seen dimly through a dreamy haze. Aye, now we were more than conquerors!

Maybe death is like this. A long, painful struggle, and what appears to be the end of all things: a tightening of the throat, dimming vision . . . the fading away of familiar and well-loved faces . . . a sinking into a vast abyss . . . thick, velvety darkness . . . and, after that—the Light!

> I will lift up mine eyes unto the mountains:
> From whence shall my help come?
> My help cometh from the Lord,
> Who made heaven and earth. [ASV]

"For I am persuaded, that neither death, nor life, nor angels, nor principalities, nor powers, nor things present, nor things to come, nor height, nor depth, nor any other creature, shall be able to separate us from the love of God, which is in Christ Jesus our Lord."

> Meantime the silent lip,
> Meantime the climbing feet.

2

On Losing and Finding God

Verily thou art a God that hidest thyself,
O God of Israel, the Saviour.

ISAIAH 45:15

O N FIRST inspection this text does not seem to ring true. It appears to be inaccurate and misleading. It startles and perplexes us. Why should God hide Himself? However, on sober reflection this statement appears in a softer light. By and by the text "thou art a God that hidest thyself" commends itself as not only true, but also immeasurably comforting and reassuring. Moreover, the truth of it is clearly demonstrated by experience.

I

There is an explanation at hand why this text seems, on the surface, at least, false and misleading. Have we not been taught, line upon line and precept upon precept, that God is a God who reveals Himself? Has not this truth been the theme of thousands of pulpits, classrooms, and also of innumerable books? Still more important is the fact that the Bible, and the New Testament in particular, shouts from the housetops that God has shown us His "reconciling face."

We have been taught that God has revealed Himself in nature, thus the nineteenth Psalm opens with these words: "The heavens declare the glory of God; and the firmament showeth his handiwork. Day unto day uttereth speech, and night unto night showeth knowledge." This is a favorite theme of the poets. There is a grand passage in Alexander Pope's "Essay on Man," and one much admired:

36

Ask for what end the heavenly bodies shine,
Earth for whose use? Pride answers, " 'Tis for mine:
For me kind Nature wakes her genial power,
Suckles each herb, and spreads out every flower;
Annual for me, the grape, the rose renew
The juice nectareous, and the balmy dew;
For me, the mine a thousand treasures brings;
For me, health gushes from a thousand springs;
Seas roll to waft me, suns to light me rise;
My footstool earth, my canopy the skies."

This is superb poetry, but considered as theology it is not so good. What about earthquakes, cyclones, tidal waves, venomous reptiles, man-eating tigers, the lightning's deadly stroke? In nature God is seen as a great artist, but scarcely as a loving Father.

Also, we have been taught that God has revealed Himself in His laws, and that is true. There is the law of seedtime and harvest; the law of cause and effect; and the moral law is hard as nails. The way of the transgressor is still hard. Ponder these awful lines in Edgar Allan Poe's somber poem "The Raven":

"Take thy beak from out my heart, and take thy form from
off my door!"
Quoth the Raven, "Nevermore."

We reap as we sow. "Two things," says Immanuel Kant, "fill the mind with admiration and awe, the starry heavens above and the moral law within."

Then, too, God has revealed Himself in history. Looking over the record of the centuries, despite man's inhumanity to man, there can be traced, to paraphrase Matthew Arnold, a power not of man that made for righteousness. Sometimes this is but dimly seen; again, it is written in large letters, so that he who runs may read. Surely God is revealing Himself now in the tragic breakup of the nations which have mocked His laws. And the end is not yet.

Supremely, God has revealed Himself in His Son. Recall the opening verses of the Epistle to the Hebrews, "God, who at sundry times and in divers manners spake in time past unto the fathers by the prophets, hath in these last days spoken unto us by his Son." And, again, the opening chapter of the Gospel according to John, "And the Word was made flesh, and dwelt among us (and we beheld his glory, the glory as of the only begotten of the Father), full of grace and truth."

The teaching that God is a God who reveals Himself has been proclaimed, emphasized, argued and bountifully illustrated. But there have been comparatively few to instruct us that God is a God who hides Himself. Pascal, however, a thinker of repute, is quoted as saying, "Scripture says that God is a God who hides Himself. God thus being hidden, every religion which does not say that God is hidden, is not the true religion." And there is William Cowper's cheerful stanza:

> Judge not the Lord by feeble sense,
> But trust Him for His grace.
> Behind a frowning providence
> He hides a smiling face.

We must beware of half truths; God is a God who both reveals and hides Himself.

II

It sounds irreverent to say that God plays "hide and seek" with us, but sometimes it seems that He does. This thing of finding and losing God, and then finding Him again, is a high adventure and more or less continuous. Jesus said, "Seek, and ye shall find," and St. Paul, His ambassador, speaking to a critical audience at Athens, advised his hearers to "Seek God, if haply they might feel after him and find him, though he is not far from each one of us." This is consoling theology, and to "feel," or grope, after God is the experience of a great host. It is doubtful if any two seekers ever found God in precisely the same way.

It is time to get down to cases, and see how three fellow pilgrims found God. The interviews that follow are not imaginary, but cases known to me personally: Charles, Emma and John. I say to Charles, a merchant, "How did you find God?"

Charles answers: "I come from a religious home. I think I first found God at my mother's side, where I knelt, night after night, as a little boy. I think, too, I found God in the Bible, which was read regularly in our home and which I soon learned to read for myself. Then I was taken to church at an early age, was a faithful attendant at the church school, and in my twelfth year I made a confession of faith and was received into the church. I think I can truthfully say that I found God in the home, in the Bible, in the church, and in the lives of my parents, who were consistently, devoutly and beautifully religious."

I turn next to Emma, a schoolteacher, and I say to her, "How did you find God?"

Emma replies: "I am a product of an unhappy home life; my father and mother were not happily married, and I grew up in the midst of family quarrels. In my eighth year my mother divorced my father, who soon remarried. My mother took a position and I was taken into the home of her parents, where I was reared. My mother, removed to another state and eventually remarried, wished to take me, but my grandparents, to whom I had become greatly attached, urged me to remain with them. They made a good home for me and saw that I had an excellent education. I became a teacher in one of the city schools. The principal of this school was an exceptionally fine character, a religious man, and he took a special interest in me, overlooked some of my early mistakes, and helped me to become an effective teacher. The early experiences in my unhappy home left their mark on me, and I fought hard against a tendency to cynicism and a distrust of humanity. I had no interest in religion except to be mildly critical of churches and church people. But all the time the influence of the fine character of the principal was telling on my life. After several years as a teacher I married an estimable young man and our home life was ideal. But we lost our first child while still a baby, and into our bereft home came this principal to sit with us and impart the Christian view of death. He was so kind and understanding and so helpful that the terrible blow we had sustained was softened. One Sunday my husband and I slipped into a pew in the church where the principal held membership and was an active leader. To shorten a long story, we united with that church, and are happy and contented in this new relationship. I think I shall have to answer, I found God in the fine, sympathetic character of my school principal."

I say to John, a lawyer, "How did you find God?" He replies: "I found God through a hard soul-searching struggle. My family were religious people, not ardently so, but were, at least nominally, church members. I am of a skeptical nature. I have a tough mind. I seek proof and evidence; you see, I am a lawyer by training and profession. Early in my practice I faced a crisis and a huge disappointment. I felt I had been cheated out of life's great prize. The years passed and I came to realize that nothing could have been worse for me than to have won the prize I coveted. This awakening, if I may call it such, set me to thinking deeply about religion and Christianity in particular. I gave the New Testament a close study. I read the best books I could find both for and against the ancient Faith. I came at last to a conviction that the teachings of Christ were supreme. No, I am not yet a church member, although I may become such some day. I believe that God is, and that He is a rewarder of those who seek Him. I found God through a crisis and through a long period of study, earnest thought, and, yes, I'll say it, I found God in my heart."

Now it will be seen in these interviews, which I think are

representative, that in two of the cases God was hidden for a while, that the teacher and the lawyer found Him only after certain harrowing experiences, and at last the clouds lifted and they saw the Light and basked in its genial warmth. I do not assume that Charles, Emma and John, and a host of other believers, were ever without seasons of clouds so thick that they could not see God clearly and were obliged to walk by faith until the clouds rolled away and they again sensed His presence. Life is like that, even the life of faith. The hidden God is the same just and merciful God as the God revealed. "Verily thou art a God that hidest thyself."

Now, there are other roads to God in addition to the ways in which Charles, Emma and John found Him. Some of the ways are past searching out. Sometimes men and women have found God through the fragrance of a flower which awakened long-slumbering memories; through the hearing of a half-forgotten melody which vibrated a deep note; or, perchance, it was the smile on the face of a little child; or, again, it was a letter or a telephone call; maybe through a shock, a loss, a gain. Myriad are the ways by which we find God and He finds us.

III

I come now to a tender and revealing episode within the life of the church I served for twenty-six years, an incident which confirms the truth of my text, "Thou art a God that hidest thyself." It concerns one of the most devoted Christian gentlemen it has been my good fortune to know, the late Fletcher Sears. Mr. Sears was singularly gifted in public prayer. He read the Bible through, year after year, thirty-two times in all. He was great in his simplicities. He had but three interests, his church, his home and his business. For fifty years he was the purchasing agent of the Detroit and Cleveland Navigation Company. Theologically, he was a Conservative—spelled with a capital letter. He and I did not live precisely in the same world

theologically, but we did in the world of the Spirit, which is, I
think, more fundamental. He respected and loved me, and I in
turn reciprocated respect and affection for him.

Mr. and Mrs. Sears were a distinguished couple. They stood
out uniquely from the rest of us. Mr. Sears was always impec-
cably attired, and carried himself with a kind of old-world
courtesy—when the old world was at its best. Mrs. Sears was
tall, willowy and a gracious person. That they were childless is
a fact which may have had bearing on their strait-laced Puritan
manner of life. Mr. Sears had never so much as seen a theatrical
performance, a motion picture or a professional baseball game.
He did not know one playing card from another, and as for
dancing, he was a stranger even to the old-fashioned Virginia
reel. Yet, he was not a "kill-joy," nor wanting in a sense of
humor, and could chuckle over the telling of a good, clean story.
At church Mr. and Mrs. Sears sat well up toward the front,
eloquent listeners to the sermon, and especially so if they
deemed it doctrinally sound. During the celebration of the
Communion of the Lord's Supper their worshipful mood was of
commingled humility and adoration. For many years Mr. Sears
taught the Alpha Bible Class, which was composed of mature
churchwomen who, as they listened to their teacher unfold the
Holy Scriptures, were "lost in wonder, love and praise."

After a long life, singularly free from sickness, Fletcher Sears
was stricken with a painful ailment which necessitated surgery
and heroic treatment, long drawn out. During this period,
Mrs. Sears, on one of her daily visits to her husband, fell, frac-
turing her hip, and was destined to be a patient in another
hospital for the rest of her life. Thus, the skies darkened for
these devout children of God, and the time of Sunset and Evening Star drew on apace.

Never shall I forget my last visit to Mr. Sears not long before
his passing. I was about to leave the city for some engagements,
to be gone for a month, so I sought him out as he lay fighting
pain and loneliness. He looked at me earnestly, felt for my hand

and clasped it eagerly. "How are you today, dear friend?" I inquired. He gave me a searching gaze, and addressing me formally as was his wont, said slowly and sadly, "Doctor Jones, I have lost God in this long illness. Yes, I have lost God. I know I am a saved man because I have done all the things the Lord commanded, but I have lost Him in this pain and suffering."

My clasp on his hand tightened and a brooding silence fell upon us. Then something moved me to say, ever so gently, "My friend, you are in grand company." "What do you mean by that," he inquired, pain and incredulity written large upon his face. "I mean this: Job, in his experience of pain and loss, lost God for a while. Do you not recall that he said 'Oh that I knew where I might find him! that I might come even to his seat!' Then, Jeremiah had a similar experience and cried out that he had lost God. And, above all, our Lord in one terrible moment on the cross lost God, and cried, 'My God, my God, why hast thou forsaken me?' And there are others. You are in the best of company—saints of God."

The sick man's clasp on my hand increased in pressure and a ghost of a smile played about his lips. "Of course you are right! I wonder how I forgot that. Maybe the pain clouded my mind. Now I want you to pray with me before you leave." And when I said good-by to Fletcher Sears that day it was "good-by" until we meet again on that Farther Shore. "Verily thou art a God that hidest thyself"—not sparing any of Thy children, no matter how faithful.

IV

I am not quite through. I am fond of dogs. In my day we have had a mongrel, two cockers, a poodle, and now a Dalmatian, or "coach dog," as the breed is commonly known. The Dalmatian is a noble dog, stately and affectionate. Sometimes I think my Prince, religiously, is a Presbyterian, so proper and dignified he is. Politically, I think he must be a Republican, since, during the last Presidential election, when I took him for his walk, he wanted to go into every big white house we passed. Curiously this large, powerful dog becomes frightened by any unusual noise. The backfiring of an automobile or a thunderstorm sends him all atremble to his master or mistress. I find it difficult to account for his plight. Perhaps Prince is gun-shy, or it may be it is the fear of the unknown which transforms him into a frightened and bewildered creature.

One May day a few years ago I was in my upstairs study when a thunderstorm suddenly broke over us. Almost immediately Prince came up the stairs, trembling violently. He attempted to get up on my knees, and I pushed him from me gently. Instantly he went berserk, sprang upon me with terrific force and sank two fangs into my arm. I cannot describe adequately my surprise and shock. I stood up unsteadily, called a taxi and went to a doctor's office, where the wound was cauterized and I was given an antitetanus shot.

No, I didn't punish my dog, I *forgave* him. You see, we are gods to our dogs. They know nothing so wonderful and so beneficent as their masters or mistresses. Our dogs worship us. My dog came to me in his distress and I cast him off. His god had forsaken him in his dire need and in a moment of anguish he turned against me. I treated my dog as I hope the Heavenly Father will treat me if ever in a fit of terror or despondency I decide that He has cast me off and turn against Him. "Verily thou art a God that hidest thyself, O God of Israel, the Saviour."

3

Magnificent Reminders

And he spake unto the children of Israel, saying, When your children shall ask their fathers in time to come, saying, What mean these stones? then ye shall let your children know, saying, Israel came over this Jordan on dry land.

JOSHUA 4:21, 22

And he took bread, and when he had given thanks, he brake it, and gave to them, saying, This is my body which is given for you: this do in remembrance of me.

LUKE 22:19 (ASV)

THERE is in these two fragments of Scripture, one from the Old and the other from the New Testament, a sorry commentary on a human frailty—our proneness to forget what we ought to remember. How could the children of Israel ever forget their passing through the river Jordan "as by dry land"? But, they did! How could these children of bondage when freed from shackles forget the manner of their deliverance or the beneficence of the Deliverer? But, they did! How can an enlightened people forget Jesus Christ, His coming to redeem humanity, and the sacrifice He made upon the Cross? But, they do!

The Eternal Father, who "knoweth our frame," knows how easily we forget. In some respects so-called "dumb" animals have better and longer memories than human beings. The elephant is said never to forget either a kindness or an injury; and a dog, seldom. But man's memory needs a lot of jogging. We are a nation of forgetters, and it is a wise provision that appoints seasons and raises monuments such as revive sluggish memories and stimulate the imagination. It is the exceptional generation that recognizes and rewards justly its noblest leaders while they are alive. Time and perspective seem necessary. After prejudice and calumny have done their worst, at a later day Justice and Good Will come to court.

Far in front the cross stands ready and the crackling faggots burn,
While the hooting mob of yesterday in
Silent awe return to glean up the scattered ashes
Into History's golden urn.

Monuments, memorials, shrines, anniversaries, celebrations—all have their warrant in the melancholy fact that we are a forgetful people. Some of these memorials may be fittingly described as Magnificent Reminders.

Take our nation's history and the anniversaries, celebrations, monuments which recall to us rememberable events and personages. At the capital of our Republic are Magnificent Reminders of two men whom it seemed the Lord raised up to match the hour and the event. One of these Magnificent Reminders is a tall, plain shaft, 555 feet in height, towering above the city, a colossal finger pointing to the sky. It is sacred to the memory of him of whom it was said he was "first in war, first in peace, and first in the hearts of his countrymen," and of whom another said, "Nature left him childless, that his country might call him Father."

The second Magnificent Reminder is at the west end of the Mall, where stands a white marble temple, beautiful in design and of Doric simplicity. Inside is the statue by French of a brooding figure sitting at ease in the great chair. The expression on the deeply lined face is one in which kindness and sadness are mingled. This is the memorial to the man who preserved the Union and of whom a eulogist has said, "He is the gentlest memory of our world."

There is a third Magnificent Reminder. It is the statue of a recumbent General Robert E. Lee, at Lexington, Virginia. The General, fully accoutered in his uniform, lies in marble effigy. He appears to be asleep, having lain down for a needed rest.

The discerning, reverent visitor steps softly, lest he wake the sleeping soldier. That statue, the work of the sculptor Valentine, who put his best into the impressive monument, is a Magnificent Reminder of a very great gentleman, who was never greater than in the defeat which he transformed into a victory of moral grandeur.

I

The Eternal God has seen fit to give us certain Magnificent Reminders that He is, and that He is a rewarder of them that seek Him. One of these is the ancient Jewish Sabbath and the Christian Sunday or the Lord's Day.

It is doubtful if Judaism could have survived had it not been for the Sabbath institution and celebration. The Sabbath holds a place of vast importance in the Bible. The commandment to keep the Sabbath Day holy is the fourth in the Decalogue. Jerusalem fell in 586 B.C. The Temple was destroyed and the people were taken into Babylon as captives. Those were dark days, and it seemed as though the candle of the Jewish people was extinguished. But there went with the captives the prophet Ezekiel, and he made the observance of the Sabbath of primary importance. Once a week these captive people stood up to be counted. It was their Holy Day and they kept it in solemn celebration with prayer and praise. No matter that all around them the practices of Babylon prevailed. No matter whether there were taunts and ridicule from their captors. These exiled Jews kept the Sabbath Day, and the Sabbath Day kept them.

The best days of our own nation are those when we keep the Christian Sunday or Lord's Day in a reverent and becoming manner. In days gone by some of us can remember a serenity and peace which seemed to fall over the land when the Lord's Day dawned. On the farm the livestock rested in stall and field. The people from the countryside put on their best clothes and drove miles to some plain meetinghouse to fix their thoughts upon God, the reading of the Holy Scriptures and "Her sweet

communion, solemn vows." They sang the hymns that were
dear to them and for the while they forgot the toil and the
struggle, the anxiety and the disappointment. Heaven seemed
near by. Life took on a new and grander meaning. They felt
themselves to be children of the Heavenly Father and that He
stood within the shadow keeping watch above His own.

> O day of rest and gladness,
> O day of joy and light:
> O balm of care and sadness,
> Most beautiful most bright!

It is a sad mistake to think we have outgrown this "day of all
the week the best," this Magnificent Reminder that God is and
that He is the rewarder of them that seek Him. Is it not true that
even those who feel themselves to have outgrown institutional
religion would not wish to live in a land where every day was
like every other day, a land where there were no religious services, no day of physical and mental rest, no day designed to
quicken the spiritual nature? If this day were to go out of
existence, something would go out of our lives; something fine
and noble perish from the earth.

The early Christians replaced the Jewish Sabbath, which was
the seventh day, with the Christian's first day of the week, a
standing memorial to the Gospel of the Empty Tomb and of
Him Who ever liveth to intercede. In our eagerness to emphasize
the resurrection and the gift of eternal life on Easter, we have
unintentionally played down the fact that every Sunday, every
Lord's Day, is a memorial, an anniversary of that stupendous
event. Every Sunday it is fitting to sing, "He is risen, He is risen,
Tell it out with joyful voice." When John, the beloved disciple,
was exiled to the Isle of Patmos, he remembered this day of days
and wrote down, for millions to read who should come after him,
that he was in the Spirit on the Lord's Day. That is a fine phrase,
"in the Spirit on the Lord's Day." He must have meant that he
was sensitive to spiritual impulses, his thoughts purified and

exalted, his passions subdued, his purposes ennobled, his vision enlarged and sharpened, his heart warmed, his whole being suffused and energized with the Spirit of God. The Lord's Day can do the same for every worshiping soul.

Once a week, O fellow pilgrims, God gives us this Magnificent Reminder of His unspeakable Gift to the world. To be "in the Spirit on the Lord's Day" should mean that the other days of the week will be used wisely, helpfully, and not only to oneself, but to fellow pilgrims along the way. A Magnificent Reminder is the Lord's Day, a red-letter day in the calendar of Christendom.

> Yes, child of suffering, thou mayest well be sure,
> He who ordained the Sabbath loved the poor.

II

Another Magnificent Reminder that God is and that He is a rewarder of them that seek Him is the Synagogue of the Jews and the Church of our Christian Faith.

Of the Jewish institution of worship I speak now only a passing word, but it should profit us to remember that in Babylonian exile, when the Sabbath was reinstated, the Synagogue came into existence, the replica of the great Temple that stood in Jerusalem, dear to the heart of every zealous Jew. These Magnificent Reminders are linked together more closely than we think—the Sabbath and the Synagogue, Sunday or the Lord's Day and the Church of the Christ, "ground and pillar of the truth." The Church is a standing monument, a constant reminder of God, of Christ, of the life of the Spirit, of prayer as a life force and of the life eternal.

Before I leave the Synagogue I am prompted to relate my first experience in preaching for a Conservative congregation of the Jewish faith. The place was my city of Detroit, and the Synagogue, Shaarey Zedek, the largest congregation of its kind in the city. It was at the time when Adolf Hitler had let loose the fires of persecution on the Jews in Germany and massacred them by the thousands. At such a stage of modern history when many Jews in America were mourning the loss of kinspeople on the other side of the Atlantic, I was asked by the rabbi of Shaarey Zedek to preach at a regular Friday night service of worship, and accepted the invitation. I looked out over seven or eight hundred worshipers, and in the front were a dozen or so aged Jewish women, veritable Mothers in Israel. I spoke from Psalms 31:8, "Thou hast set my feet in a large room," and these were my divisions: (1) The Roominess of the Life of Faith, (2) The Illimitable Area of Prayer, (3) The Unexplored Territories of Spiritual Fellowship, and (4) The Untrammeled Plateaus of the Immortal Hope.

When I had finished with the sermon and the benediction had been pronounced, the rabbi asked me to step down from the pulpit and meet some of his people. First to greet me were the Mothers in Israel mourning for relatives who had perished in the furnace of persecution. The first of these to greet me took my hand, bowed low over it, and, as she did so, a hot tear rolled down her cheek and splashed upon my hand. I was deeply touched, and then and there I had a sign and seal of a new understanding of the tie that binds in sorrow and loss all God's children in one family. Verily the Jewish Synagogue is a Magnificent Reminder that God is, and that He is a rewarder of them that seek Him.

I would have you know that when I speak of the Church I am not referring solely to this church nor to the churches down or up the street, but to all the churches which compose the Church Universal—churches of every description, little and great, rural and urban, rich and poor, the churches in this and every land. The Church is greater than the churches. The churches are but broken lights of the Church—some very much broken—yet all churches, congregations, chapels, meetinghouses, cathedrals are Magnificent Reminders, I repeat, that God is, and that He is a rewarder of them that seek Him.

Every once in a while a minister, unwisely, I think, preaches

on "Why Don't More People Go to Church?" Rather, his subject should be "Why Do So Many People Go to Church?"
Think of it: there are many other places to which one may go
of a more entertaining nature, where he is freer to move about
and do as he pleases. As Harry Lauder used to sing, "Oh it's nice
to get up in the morning, but it's nicer to lie in bed." It is often
a privation to leave a comfortable house on a cold or storm-swept
day to attend a church several miles distant. Nevertheless, all
over this nation and other lands people continue to go to church
in season and out of season. The surprising thing is not that
attendance at public worship is dying out, but that it is very
much alive. Churches are ubiquitous; theaters, baseball fields
and race tracks are not.

III

To the reverent-minded even an empty church building has
a fascination and a meaning all its own. I love to step into such
buildings (alas, I have been locked out more than once) and
muse awhile amid the silence and the memories which such an
experience evokes. For a new edifice, no matter how spacious,
costly, or beautiful, is wanting the mystic meaning the place
will have when it has housed a congregation for half a century
or more. The sculptural years that chisel eloquent lines in
human faces impart a like distinction to humble chapels and
mighty cathedrals.

Some years ago I spent a night in a hotel at Douglas, Isle of
Man. In the morning, after breakfast, I remarked to the clerk
at the desk that I was going out for a long walk and asked if
there was anything worth seeing within that radius. "Yes," he
replied, "about a mile from here is a church in which John
Wesley once preached." I thanked him and set out to see that
church. The August day was serenely perfect, and the near-by
Irish Sea sparkled like acres of diamonds. By and by I came in
sight of the church, a small brick building. I stood in front of it
and read the inscription that on a certain date "John Wesley

preached here." I tried the door, but to my dismay it was locked. Presently I found a window through which I could view the pulpit where John Wesley once stood up to preach. As I gazed upon that pulpit I recalled that I had somewhere read that when John Wesley died, all that he left behind was "a few books, a worn pulpit gown—and the Methodist Church!"

A church building which has weathered many years is eloquent, the empty edifice redolent with "memories that bless and burn." Thus Hannah Kahn's poem on "An Old Church" is suffused with a tenderness too deep for tears:

> The walls which now
> Are crumbling lime
> Could not withstand
> The urge of time.
>
> The wood has rotted
> On the doors;
> Rain has ravished
> Roof and floors. . . .
>
> And yet because
> Men worshipped here,
> Something Holy
> And austere
>
> Lingers on
> And fills the air,
> Like echoes
> Of a quiet prayer.

IV

There are two ordinances, according to the New Testament, sometimes called "sacraments": baptism and the Lord's Supper. There is a far-reaching significance to these ordinances. They are not merely rites, not solely ceremonies. Christian baptism is a dramatic reminder; an outward sign of an inward grace. In Romans, the sixth chapter, we read in the third and fourth verses, "Or are ye ignorant that all we who were baptized into

Christ Jesus were baptized into his death? We were buried therefore with him through baptism into death: that like as Christ was raised from the dead through the glory of the Father, so we also might walk in newness of life" (ASV). A baptism following the manner practiced in the days when the Church was young, when it is administered with dignity and solemnity, is an impressive ceremony. It is pictorial, dramatic. It represents death, burial and resurrection. Christian baptism, whatever the form, when done decently and in order, is solemn, beautiful, helpful.

The second ordinance is the memorial feast, the Holy Communion or, as it is called in the New Testament, the Lord's Supper. It is a love-drenched reminder that God is not willing that any shall perish but all find new life in His Son, and that, abundantly. An eminent Christian leader has said that the reunion of the divided Church will come at the table of the Lord, where the loaf and the cup, the bread and the wine, remind us so ineffably of that badge of discipleship by which all men shall know that we are Christ's disciples. The Catholic Church puts the Mass at the center of worship, and the Mass has at its base the simple observance traced in the Gospel record. The Greek Church does the same with even more elaborate ceremonies. The Lutherans and the Episcopalians put the Eucharist, which is but another name for the Lord's Supper, a name meaning "solemn feast of thanksgiving," into the center of their worship. For there is something in this ordinance which gets at the heart of the Gospel.

> Love divine, all love excelling,
> Joy of heaven, to earth come down.

One of the able ministers of the Presbyterian Church and long the preacher of old St. Andrews, Toronto, the Reverend Dr. J. R. P. Sclater, makes eight affirmations with regard to what he calls the Sacrament of the Lord's Supper: (1) A Memorial Feast; (2) A Sacrificial Feast; (3) A Method of Teaching

Truth by Symbol; (4) The Sign of a Fixed Agreement; (5) The Chief Thanksgiving Occasion of the Church; (6) The Family Meal of the Church; (7) Attendance at the Celebration Is a Badge of Christian Discipleship; (8) It Is the Prophecy of the Perfected Kingdom. Surely the Lord's Supper is a Magnificent Reminder that God is, that Jesus Christ died for all mankind, that prayer is potent, love dynamic and faith the victory!

These two ordinances are part and parcel of the Church. Not for one moment do I believe that these ordinances can of themselves be substituted for the kind of life which they symbolize, but they have their place and power and authority. It is best to use them discerningly, reverently, gratefully, and pass on to the noble way of life they symbolize, "That life, which is life indeed."

We sometimes speak of the Church as demanding this or that of us. It is just as true, and in a sense truer, that something within us, deep down, demands the Church do something for us. With the Greeks who came to Philip, we too exclaim, "Sir, we would see Jesus." We are such a needy people and so forgetful. We need to be reminded of what we were, what we now are and what by the grace of God we may yet become! It is wrong to belittle church attendance, a mistake to say one can worship anywhere. It isn't true that one may worship God in His great out-of-doors, on the mountainside or beside the sea just as helpfully as he can worship God within four walls of a building dedicated to the Most High. Such a one may find much to praise God for as he gazes upon His handiwork, and that is good. But there is no adequate substitute for public worship where men, women and little children can congregate to learn of God and His Son, our Saviour. The Church, and only the Church, provides such a place. It puts us in remembrance of the fundamental themes of the Faith which no gathering of a purely secular nature can do. The Church's primary concern is with God and man, the forgiveness of sin, the new life of the Spirit, the Christlikeness of the forgiving spirit, and the sharing of one's life with the Eternal and with His children. What other institution does this? Not one!

Sometimes one hears it said: "What do I get out of the Church?" The answer is, "How much do you put in, not only of what you have but of what you are?" So much depends on what we bring to the Church and public worship in spirit, mind and heart. What we take away depends so largely on what we bring to the Church: receptivity of spirit, eloquent listening, contrite hearts, willingness to learn and to share, a disposition to aspire.

Dr. Fosdick holds that the next great conflict will be between Christianity and communism. That battle of ideas and principles is on. The two systems are in conflict in both belief and practice. They have some things in common. Both are international in scope and both profess to believe in the brotherhood of man, although they differ in the method of its realization. Christianity believes in the priority of the spiritual; communism in the priority of the economic or materialistic. If Christianity is to win a moral victory over communism, our Christianity will have to be more enthusiastic, more zealous, more generous, more aggressive than it now is; and we must also have unity of purpose and of spirit. Russian communists have what they would call a Magnificent Reminder in the memory of Lenin, their illustrious leader. His lifeless body is carefully guarded at Moscow and is a shrine to which the Russians repair from time to time for rededication to their purposes and program.

Our Magnificent Reminder is the spiritual body of Christ, His living Church. What homage do we pay to Christ's memory, the incomparable saga of His earthly life, the victories of the risen Christ? If we treat the Magnificent Reminders God has given us—the Lord's Day and the Church—with anything short of the loyalty and devotion that communists give to their ideals, principles and objectives, they will outstrip us in economic missionary zeal, passion and spirit of sacrifice for their political system.

Of the imperfections of the churches, and particularly of my own, I am painfully aware. To the foibles and follies of the saints I am not a stranger. Defects, lapses from rectitude, indiscretions, wrongdoings—these describe our common lot wherever cast. The Church is not a spiritual aristocracy nor an exclusive club. It is for imperfect human beings who dare to press on to perfection. It is for sinners like you and me. We humbly confess our need of the Magnificent Reminders that God is, and that He is a rewarder of them that seek Him.

O, Magnificent Reminders lest we forget. For things are going badly with our old world. It is doubtful if in any period of history of which we have any record there was such a dire need for spiritual renewal. Let the greatly loved old hymn speak for us what our poor stammering lips, unaided, cannot say in so many words, or so beautifully:

> I love Thy kingdom, Lord,
> The house of Thine abode,
> The Church our blest Redeemer saved
> With His own precious blood.
>
> I love Thy Church, O God!
> Her walls before Thee stand,
> Dear as the apple of Thine eye,
> And graven on Thy hand.
>
> For her my tears shall fall,
> For her my prayers ascend,
> To her my cares and toils be given,
> Till toils and cares shall end.

4

The Peace of Great Phantoms

So great a cloud of witnesses.
HEBREWS 12:1

SOME years ago Carl Sandburg autographed one of his
Lincoln books for me and included this sentiment: "May
the peace of Great Phantoms be for you." The majestic phrase
impressed me deeply, and never since has it been long out of my
thoughts. I planted it in what I call my Sermon Garden, which
I locate in some nook or corner of my mind. But, unlike some
sermonic seeds I drop in this garden, its growth was slow, and
required favorable conditions to come to time of bud and blos-
som. Nor am I sure, even after years of brooding over the poet's
inscription, I can do justice to the thoughts that lie too deep for
an adequate treatment of the theme. What I needed was an
experience, episode or event that would provide the insight and
inspiration for which I had long waited.

I

For many years our household has summered at Campbell
Park, near Pentwater, Michigan. This ideal spot for vacationing
was purchased and laid out nearly fifty years ago by a group of
noted ministers, university professors, editors and a few eminent laymen, members of the communion known as Disciples of
Christ. The neat and comfortable cottages are built high up on
sand dunes, with a background of woodland in which pine and
hemlock predominate. The cottages face a grand sweep of Lake
Michigan, with the long freighters passing, silhouetted against
the ever-changing sky.

The summer of 1952, we took over in "Bethany Cottage,"

built and long occupied by the H. L. Willett family. Both Dr. and Mrs. Willett have passed into "that life which is life indeed," leaving precious memories of gracious living and beautiful friendships. The cottage today is as it was when the Willetts were in residence there. On the walls are tapestries and pictures brought from the Near and Far East, to which this scholar-orator had journeyed seven times or more. Some four hundred of Dr. Willett's books are in the cottage, and with these we kept high company.

One day, in browsing among the volumes in his "bedside library," to quote a phrase beloved by the late Dr. Alexander Whyte of Edinburgh, I came across the Bible which Dr. Willett had so intimately used in the days when he was ranked as one of the most gifted lecturers and preachers on the American scene, appearing often at Chautauqua, New York, Winona Lake, Indiana, and in many other important assemblies. Handling this Bible reverently and with an absorbing interest, I found it plentifully marked, carefully annotated, and with marginal notes in the owner's familiar script. There were also outlines of certain of his finest lectures deftly inserted between the pages. Such a diligently and intelligently marked Bible I had never seen before, nor do I ever expect to see another like it. As I turned the leaves and reflected on some comment my honored friend had noted, I seemed to see the gifted scholar and hear again the accents of his matchless voice; when he had concluded a lecture or sermon, it was "like the ceasing of exquisite music." There, in that well-remembered home where I had so often been a guest of the Willetts, the peace of Great Phantoms was for me, and Sandburg's impressive words took on a new and fuller meaning.

Late that night I strolled alone through Campbell Park. A waxing moon bathed the dunes and beach in silver, and the waves gently lapping the shore made soft music. Great Phantoms accompanied me. Ministering spirits sent forth to comfort and ennoble kept step with me and, although I was by myself, I was not alone: so great a cloud of witnesses were around and about me. It was this ineffable experience which leads me now to explore farther Sandburg's phrase, upon which I have so long mused and dreamed.

II

The peace of Great Phantoms! There have been times when this peace fell upon us as we tarried in some vast library and gazed longingly upon the high tiers and almost endless shelves of storied volumes—gazed until it seemed we were in the very presence of the illustrious masters of prose, poetry, history, biography and drama—what a royal company and how real they were—"those immortal dead, who live again in minds made better by their presence." In truth, a book lover's first impression of a huge and famous library, such as the Bodleian at Oxford, the Library of Congress at Washington, or the Huntington in California, is one of bewilderment, followed by a sense of dismay on realizing how few of the volumes in the colossal collection he knows or ever will know. By and by this commingled sense of bewilderment and dismay gives place to another—the peace of Great Phantoms; and then the enraptured visitor becomes conscious of a shining host, not only of the renowned authors themselves but also of the characters they made so famous: Shakespeare and Hamlet; Hawthorne and the Reverend Arthur Dimmesdale; Washington Irving and Rip Van Winkle; Hugo and Jean Valjean; Dickens and David Copperfield; Thackeray and Becky Sharp—these and myriad others now come to life—so great a cloud of witnesses!

Albeit even a few good books can likewise inspire this peace of Great Phantoms. Think of Lincoln brooding over his great little library: old Aesop, John Bunyan, Daniel Defoe, Parson Weems, and, best of all, the mighty characters of the Bible, a book which he knew so intimately and so well. Few of the great of Lincoln's day came his wilderness way; rather, he companied with those dead who never die. What noble Phantoms peopled his humble cabin home: Washington, Jefferson, Isaiah, Amos and Jeremiah; Peter the big fisherman, John the beloved, the mighty Paul and, supremely, Jesus, Master of us all! So great a cloud of witnesses!

Grand old John Milton knew this mystic companionship of great books and the peace such comradeship brings. "For books are not absolutely dead things," he wrote, "but do contain a potency of life in them to be as active as that soul was whose progeny they are; nay, they do preserve as in a vial of purest efficacy an extraction of that living intellect that bred them. . . . Many a man lives a burden to the earth; but a good book is the precious lifeblood of a master spirit embalmed and stored up on purpose to a life beyond life!"

Longfellow was aware of that peace of which I speak when, in verses addressed to Robert Burns, he wrote:

> His presence haunts this room to-night . . .
> From that far coast.
> Welcome beneath this roof of mine!
> Welcome! this vacant chair is thine,
> Dear guest and ghost.

So great a cloud of witnesses!

III

A burial ground, "God's acre," is favorable to the peace of Great Phantoms, nor need it be a vast city cemetery, where the dust of celebrities rests beneath marble splendor. One of the most widely known poems in the English language was inspired by a rural churchyard where "the rude forefathers of the hamlet sleep." In such a quiet pastoral scene, "far from the madding crowd's ignoble strife," Thomas Gray found the material for his "Elegy Written in a Country Church-yard." The phantoms that people that sequestered spot and bring peace to the musing visitant are obscure heroes, peasants and yeomanry whose names were unknown to fame. They lived, loved, suffered, served, "died and made no sign." Yet, remembering their virtues and homely toil, the brooding poet sensed the presence of Great Phantoms and gave their as yet unheralded fidelities a sure immortality.

> For thee, who, mindful of th' unhonour'd dead
>> Dost in these lines their artless tale relate;
> If chance, by lonely contemplation led,
>> Some kindred spirit shall inquire thy fate.

And what shall be said of the Westminster Abbeys, the Père Lachaises, Pantheons, Arlingtons, Oak Ridges, Forest Lawns, Cave Hills, Mount Vernons and Monticellos, to which multitudes pilgrimage to muse and dream and pray? Poets, painters, dramatists, novelists, statesmen, soldiers, sailors, merchant princes, philosophers, fair ladies of yesteryear, phantoms all. Some found a peace in death they never knew in life. If some come to these places of lonely contemplation and weep, God grant that they shall weep in peace.

And Gettysburg! Here is one of the saddest shrines in all America. To wander over that wide expanse where Pickett's men marched to what the world calls glory, or climb storied hilltops where men died in shambles, is to company with phantom heroes while the voice of memory whispers low, "If you have tears, prepare to shed them now." The blood of contending armies, both American, hallows the ground where brave men gave their last full measure of devotion. As in a dream, the visitor sees a tall, gaunt, lonely man standing before a multitude, speaking in simple and beautiful words a tribute to those who struggled there, and, mingling with his noble phrasings in muffled antiphonal, he hears the words of another illustrious American: "Liberty and Union, now and forever, one and inseparable!"

Sandburg, writing of Gettysburg three quarters of a century later, mused about a tall, old clock in a quiet corner of a farmhouse. The face and dial of that clock had known the eyes of a boy who listened to its tick-tock, and learned to read its minute and hour hands.

... and the people in the cottage knew that the clock would stand there and the boy never again come into the room and look at the clock with the query, "what is the time." ... In a row of graves of the unidentified dead the boy would sleep long in the dedicated resting-place at Gettysburg. Why had he gone away and why would he never come back had roots in some mystery of flags and drums, of national fate in which individuals sink as in a deep sea, of men swallowed and vanished in a man-made storm of smoke and steel.

O phantoms of Gettysburg, Suresnes, Arlington, and myriad other places where white crosses stand row on row, speak to warmongers the world around and bid them to repent and seek the paths of peace!

IV

What phantoms stride the streets and tarry in the old rendez-vous of the famed cities of the world. In the midst of his Phi Beta Kappa oration at Harvard University, June 3, 1881, Wendell Phillips told of seeing suddenly on a street in Florence, under his very feet, this inscription: "On this spot three hundred years ago sat Dante." As he said this, so a gentlemen who was present reported, the orator was transfigured in tone, manner and posture, so that his hearers saw what he saw. They, too, were in Florence, and Dante had come to life!

Reflect, I pray you, upon a few of the renowned streets of both the old and the new worlds: High Street, Edinburgh! Fleet Street, London! The Champs Elysées, Paris! the Via Dolorosa, Jerusalem! Fifth Avenue, New York! Market Street, San Francisco! Michigan Avenue, Chicago! Woodward Avenue, Detroit! Then there is Princes Street, Edinburgh! What a street of Great Phantoms!—Titans and Olympians. Those of us who have roamed along its broad thoroughfare can never forget our emotions as we looked about: the embattled castle frowning from the promontory, the gardens in the valley partly concealing the passing trains, the smoke drifting high above the ancient buildings. What a panorama of grandeur, ancient conflicts, great houses and shabby tenements. On this fabled street, walled on the north by massive business blocks, and facing these the proud monument in memory of Sir Walter Scott—what phantoms of yesterdays lightly tread this street of history!

Once while strolling along Princes Street I beheld the phantoms of the past. As in a dream I saw, or thought I saw, swinging along this street, a group of noble churchmen: brave old John Knox, staff in hand; Thomas Chalmers, with a faraway look in his eyes; Henry Drummond, debonair and friendly; Principal Rainy, a lordly figure; Robertson Smith, the knightly scholar; the eloquent Thomas Guthrie; and that benign Puritan, Alexander Whyte. There were others—names which glorify the Scottish church. These pass on, and, replacing them, behold the phantom forms of men of letters emerge in arresting array. Lo! Robert Burns, alone in Edinburgh and sighing for Ayr and familiar scenes; Allan Ramsay, as lonely as Burns; Sir Walter Scott, a favorite dog at his heels; ah, and there is Robert Louis Stevenson, arm-in-arm with J. M. Barrie; and dear John Watson, "Ian Maclaren" we loved to call him, of *Beside the Bonnie Brier Bush* fame; and—but here the one o'clock signal gun from the castle boomed out, and I awoke from my reveries, surrounded with passers-by in cheerful oblivion to what I saw and heard on that day of memories in Edinburgh, Scotland's pride and glory.

Vachel Lindsay, along with his brother poets, sensed the presence of Great Phantoms and the peace that flows from them. With World War I bleeding and blighting England, France, and Belgium, Lindsay, dreaming dreams and seeing visions, fancied Abraham Lincoln could not sleep in his tomb at Oak Ridge, and at midnight walked the streets of Springfield, Illinois. . . .

It is portentous, and a thing of state
That here at midnight, in our little town
A mourning figure walks, and will not rest,
Near the old court-house pacing up and down . . .

No, the mourning figure

. . . cannot rest until a spirit-dawn
Shall come;—the shining hope of Europe free:
A league of sober folk, the workers' earth,
Bringing long peace to Cornland, Alp and Sea.

For such a peace this broken world still waits, while wars thunder on. "And who will bring white peace, that he may sleep again?"

V

The homes that sheltered us in childhood days are forever places of precious memories. To journey back to these haunts of our youth is to know the peace of such priceless phantoms. For when we recall the cost of parental love and sacrifice and the lights and shadows of family life, the phantoms that take over about the old home place are truly great: great in affection, in courage, and in forgiveness.

It is recorded in the Holy Scriptures that in a stressful time of his exciting life, King David and his fighting men came to Bethlehem, place of the warrior's birth. Suddenly, as by magic, the shepherd king was back again as a youth in the old home, and he cried, "O that someone would give me to drink of the water from the well which is by the gate of Bethlehem." Persons and places of the past took over, and David was a lad again, tending his father's flocks.

When former Vice-President Adlai E. Stevenson of Bloomington, Illinois, was close to death in the Presbyterian Hospital in Chicago, he asked his nurse for a drink of water. She brought it to him. He took a sip and remarked: "This water is good, but it is not as good or cool as the water from the well on the farm in Christian County, Kentucky, where I used to drink from a gourd dipper." The peace of beloved phantoms was flooding the mind of the dying statesman.

How well Thomas Hood has described the mood which so marks "the return of the native":

> I remember, I remember
> The house where I was born,
> The little window where the sun
> Came peeping in at morn;
> He never came a wink too soon
> Nor brought too long a day;
> But now, I often wish the night
> Had borne my breath away.
>
> . . . .
>
> I remember, I remember
> The fir trees dark and high;
> I used to think their slender tops
> Were close against the sky:
> It was a childish ignorance,
> But now 'tis little joy
> To know I'm farther off from heav'n
> Than when I was a boy

When after an absence of some thirty years I returned to my boyhood scenes, I saw myself a phantom lad playing about the farmhouse in the days when

> The earth, and every common sight,
> To me did seem
> Apparelled in celestial light,
> The glory and the freshness of a dream.

VI

Churches, whether vast and ornate or plain and unadorned, and particularly old churches, are places where Great Phantoms come and go. Edgar A. Guest has a poem in which he says, "It takes a heap o' livin' in a house t' make it home." Old churches, like old books and old friends, are priceless. It is not until the newness wears off a church edifice, and the place becomes a shrine of tender and precious memories, that noble phantoms people pulpit, chancel and nave, or perchance congregate in plain meetinghouses and preaching auditoriums. The architecture is unimportant to the ministering spirits that come to church to bless and inspire. Not until marriage, birth and death have come, and joy and sorrow have brought their gifts to the altar, do those unseen worshipers greaten congregations met to praise God and to remember Jesus Christ.

Plymouth Church, Brooklyn, Trinity Church, Boston, Riverside Church, New York, Carr's Lane, Birmingham, Trinity Chapel, Brighton, are forever associated with the lives of Henry Ward Beecher, Phillips Brooks, Harry Emerson Fosdick, Robert W. Dale and Frederick Robertson. No informed and sensitive mind can worship in these churches without feeling the spiritual presence of these men who gave to these churches a power, meaning and radiance which, though intangible, is very real.

One high day I visited Plymouth Church in Brooklyn, where Henry Ward Beecher had his long and illustrious ministry. I wandered up the aisles and sat here and there in several pews. Then I went into the pulpit and stood where Beecher had poured forth a stream of exceptional eloquence and moved his hearers from tears to smiles and chuckles, then back again to serious thoughts and noble purposes. I chose a seat well up toward the front—and time shifted. . . . It is April 23, 1865, and the nation in mourning for her martyr president. Plymouth Church is filled to capacity, and hundreds clamor vainly for admittance. Henry Ward Beecher is in the midst of his sermon on "The Effects of the Death of Lincoln." He is nearing the close of an oration that held his hearers captive. "Shaking his invincible locks," he exclaims, as only Beecher could:

Dead, dead, he yet speaketh. Is Washington dead? Is Hampden dead? Is David dead? Is any man that was ever fit to live dead? Disenthralled of flesh, and risen in the unobstructed sphere where passion never comes, he begins his illimitable work. His life now is grafted on the infinite and will be fruitful as no earthly life can be. Pass on, thou that hast overcome. Your sorrows, O people, are his peace. Your bells and bands and muffled drums sound triumph in his ear. Wail and weep here; God made it echo joy and triumph there. Pass on.

And the peace of Great Phantoms was mine!

VII

What is this peace of Great Phantoms? Surely it is a peace of thanksgiving for the blessed dead who did not die in vain. It is a peace of tenderest thanksgiving for our own dear dead "loved long since and lost awhile." It is the peace of ineffable memories that come to soothe and heal and bless; memories that need to be kept green in our hearts; memories that pluck from the past stories of heroic renunciations made in behalf of righteous but unpopular causes; memories of those who, although grievously handicapped from the start, yet nevertheless fought a good fight, kept the faith, and finished the course. The peace of such memories is a peace that fortifies, heartens, edifies, and cannot be taken away, and endures to the end. It is a holy peace. God is of it and in it, a peace given not as the world gives: the peace of so great a cloud of witnesses.

Yet, the peace that Great Phantoms bring is not the peace of sheer contentment, nor is it the peace of a complacent serenity. Rather, it is the peace of high resolution and solemn dedication to the unfinished tasks of those who "died in faith, not having received the promises, but having seen them and greeted them from afar, and having confessed that they were strangers and pilgrims on the earth." For there is another side to the peace which the phantoms of the past bring to our troubled hearts, otherwise the picture is distorted and not wholly true: the peace of Great Phantoms is also a *poignant* peace and tears at the hearts of us.

Am I wrong in this? Is not the commingled pride and pain which distinguishes the eleventh of Hebrews, a chapter of Great Phantoms, justified? Can it be that the somber note that tinges Washington Irving's essay on Westminster Abbey is unwarranted? Is Mary Brent Whiteside's grave verse which follows, untrue?

> Who has known heights and depths shall not again
> Know peace—not as the calm heart knows
> Low, ivied walls; a garden close;
> The old enchantment of a rose.

No, life is like that, and so likewise is the peace of Great Phantoms. The high point is that stout hearts, no matter what life brings, can sing the "Long Meter Doxology" in ringing tones, and that the glorious "Hallelujah Chorus" was written by one who knew both heights and depths, yet dwelt upon the heights.

"So great a cloud of witnesses!"

O, mighty cloud of witnesses, open our eyes to behold, our ears to hearken, and our minds to receive.

> Dreams are they—but they are God's dreams!
> Shall we decry and scorn them?
>
> . . . .
>
> Dreams are they—to become man's dreams!*

* Thomas Curtis Clark.

5

The Farther Shore*

I HAVE brought into the pulpit this joyous Easter morning a
remarkable volume entitled *The Farther Shore*. It was presented to me by a former Detroit businessman who used to
worship in this church and helpfully contributed to the life of
the congregation in many ways. I call attention to the fact that
this book came from a businessman. Some there are who seem
reluctant to give businessmen credit for spiritual interests, hold-
ing that their ruling passion is to make money, absorbed in bank
or office or factory, giving little time or thought to spiritual
subjects. Manifestly, this is not true of all businessmen. Indeed,
the story of consecrated Christian laymen is of absorbing interest
and many are they who have place in it.

It is dangerous to generalize wrongly, yet many do, and
more's the pity! When one gets into a state of mind that leads
him to lump together all businessmen as stony-hearted, all labor
leaders as corrupt, all Jews as undesirable citizens, all Germans

---

* During my pulpit ministry I have occasionally preached a sermon
based upon a book; no, not a book review but a sermon inspired by a
notable book and yielding wondrously to homiletic use. On Easter
Sunday in 1939 I did, for me, a daring thing. I preached a sermon
based upon a volume entitled *The Farther Shore,* An Anthology of
World Opinion on the Immortality of the Soul. Moreover, I took the
book into the pulpit with me and ranged it alongside the pulpit Bible.

I may say, too, that I spent a lot of time in preparing this sermon,
condensing the material, striking a fair balance of the same and striving
to keep the sermon from dwindling into a lecture. Yes, and I worked
hard to get the content into my system, for I didn't use as much as a
single note.

Miss Mary Oliphant, my long-time secretary, urged me to expand
this sermon and bring it out in booklet form. I liked the idea, but never
got around to it. How many are the things we hoped to do but never
got around to doing! Life is like that.

as brutes, all aliens as criminals—something has happened to his reason. Actually, such a person is unreasonable, ignorant, prejudiced or all three. May we be saved from snap judgments and ready generalities.

I may remark also that the businessman who presented this volume to me is the son of a pioneer preacher who lived and died in Indiana, a rugged character, a grand old soldier of the Cross, who believed that God is and that He is a rewarder of them that seek Him. That this particular businessman is indebted to a home where religious standards were high and were maintained "through pleasant and through cloudy weather," he would readily concede and thank God for the memories of a boyhood in which Heaven and Earth mystically blended.

This book, *The Farther Shore,* is an "Anthology of World Opinion on the Immortality of the Soul." It covers a vast stretch of time, in all, a little more than four thousand years. It begins with "The Song of the Egyptian Minstrel," verses which were inscribed upon the chapel tomb of one of the Great Pyramids; and it ends with an article by Theodore Roosevelt, entitled "The Great Adventure." Within the covers of this book are the intimations of immortality as perceived by the leading thinkers, philosophers, poets and religious leaders through forty centuries. Here, grand old Homer speaks. Here, the brooding Buddha muses. Here, Pericles, the eloquent, delivers his funeral oration upon the Athenian dead. Plato, the Olympian, recalls the last days of Socrates and moralizes upon life here and hereafter. Within these pages Virgil and Horace trace the "Procession of the Gods" in imperishable lines, and Seneca, serenest of Romans, who seemed to sense the dawning of Christianity, is represented by his "Moral Essays." Marcus Aurelius sets forth his twilight thoughts and feelings about the life after death, while St. Augustine writes of the City of God. Mahomet makes his contribution to this oldest of subjects, while the Venerable Bede, Thomas Aquinas, Dante, Shakespeare, Spinoza, Fénelon, Dr. Donne, Voltaire, Immanuel Kant, Goethe, Wordsworth and

Emerson, help to swell the chorus of voices that sing of the
Farther Shore.

Then, too, the great Dr. Johnson engages in a conversation
on this subject of subjects, and the morose philosopher Schopen-
hauer sees darkly through his pessimistic spectacles. Here our
own Emerson breathes a noble optimism into his observations on
the laws of "Compensation." Tennyson, poet of immortality,
speaks in "In Memoriam" of those "altar stairs that slope through
darkness up to God." The golden-mouthed Ingersoll, standing
at the graveside of his brother, makes his own confession of faith
in words weighted with grief: "From the voiceless lips of the
unreplying dead there comes no word; but in the night of death
hope sees a star and listening Love can hear the rustle of a
wing." Here the famed Dr. Osler links hopefully science and
immortality, Sir Oliver Lodge witnesses in behalf of psychic
research and is sure that death does not end all. And last of all,
Theodore Roosevelt, still mourning over the untimely death of
his beloved son Quentin, affirms that "both Life and Death are
parts of the same great adventure."

Great old John Bunyan is here and good for ten pages—
Bunyan, whose certainty of God, immortality and the heavenly
city is so exhilarating. When Bunyan described the passing of
Mr. Valiant-for-truth through the River of Death he wrote
those words which men and women will go on repeating
through the ages to come, "So he passed over, and all the Trum-
pets sounded for him on the other side."

The Bible is royally represented in this Anthology. The finest
passages from the Book of Job, Ecclesiastes, the Book of Daniel,
the Gospel according to St. Mark, the Gospel according to
St. Luke, the fifteenth chapter of First Corinthians, and the
twenty-first and twenty-second chapters of the Revelation of
St. John the Divine. Nearly eleven pages of *The Farther Shore*
are devoted to passages from the Book of Books. The translation
used is that of the King James version, of which the editor of
that section says: "It has stood forth as the very word of God in

the minds and hearts of millions of the best educated as well as of the uneducated in every generation, including our own. Against it the waves of scholarly criticism, of scientific discovery, of theological professionalism, and of materialistic standards of well-being beat in vain."

I

My first thought as I take up this book is of the strange yet perhaps natural reticence with which we approach the subject of Death and the Beyond. For the most part, we do not refer to it until the fact has been thrust upon us by the passing of someone near and dear to us. We do not ordinarily discuss this topic in company or on social occasions. Imagine a reception or a week-end party, say, with some two dozen men and women present, and suddenly the hostess introduces the subject of the brevity of life and the certainty of death. Suppose we try to imagine the scene. We mingle with the guests at a reception. There is a murmur of many voices. The company has broken up into half a dozen groups, centering about some person or some topic of conversation. Some are discussing the latest book or play. Others are talking politics. Possibly a few are indulging in some gossipy speculation. Suddenly, the hostess calls for silence. What can this mean? Is she about to announce the engagement of her eldest daughter? Has she a pleasant surprise, some novelty in mind? Gradually, the talking ceases. The hostess waits until everyone is quiet and there is a hush of expectancy. Every eye is turned toward her. She speaks: "My dear friends, seventy-five or a hundred years from tonight where will we all be? Not here, certainly. Not in the land of the living, surely. What are we going to do about it? We are prepared to live, or think we are; but have we made any serious preparation so to live that nothing, not even death, can harm us? If we have not thought of this subject, I ask you, Why?"

Imagine such an interruption on such an occasion—if you can! The first reaction of the guests would be one of amazement.

Had their hostess lost her mind? Had she become a religious fanatic? Or was this some strange sort of practical joke she was playing upon them? And yet, despite the unusualness of such an episode—in truth, the improbability of it—if it did happen, one may believe that deep down in the hearts of the guests, however worldly, something would respond. Deep would answer deep, and in sober reflection the judgment of some of the guests would be, "It was not the occasion to bring us face to face with the inevitable experience that awaits us; but all the same, it made us think. It pulled us together abruptly. It left us a bit dazed. It sent us away not sure whether we dreamed this thing or if it really happened."

No, the deepest things of life cannot be everywhere discussed. To attempt to introduce the profoundest experiences of life in a casual conversation or on some gay outing expedition would be unseemly, admit of possible flippancy and so miss the mark altogether. But there should be times and places where these "thoughts that do often lie too deep for tears" could be calmly considered, dealt with honestly, investigated to the fullest. Intimate friends may sometimes talk them over when situations arise which introduce the subject naturally. Members of the family circle may give these thoughts their proper attention in circumstances too sacred for exploitation. Sometimes in that valley of the shadow we find light upon these deep issues of life; more often, upon the mountaintop such thoughts are suffused with a shining faith which dispels all doubts. And there is a great old Book that throws a floodlight upon these difficult problems, and those who open its pages reverently and examine them prayerfully, never read them in vain.

It is in the Church, however, where these deep subjects are sung about, prayed about, preached about. It is the Church that stands as a symbol of the Eternal in a transitory world. It is the Church which nurtures schools and classes and other groups studying lessons based upon the Old and New Testament teaching concerning the higher life. It is the Church which is designed by its very nature to inspire faith in God and the culture of the soul. It is the Church that is set to produce a people who will outthink, outlive, and outdie an unbelieving pagan society, and in so doing transform it into a dynamic brotherhood of believers, builders of the Great Hereafter in the Now.

II

My second thought, as I turn these pages, is that in any discussion of Immortality there will not be uniformity of belief or speculation. This is true even of the Bible. The Old Testament is suffused with moonlight; the New Testament is bathed in sunlight. The viewpoints of the book of Ecclesiastes and the Gospel as recorded by St. John are as different as is the weather of January from a day in June. St. Paul's view of the life beyond the grave grows, expands to the last of his writings. Interest in immortality and the desire for it fluctuate in the human heart. Some see "the farther shore" as through a mist; others behold it bathed in sunshine. Just as some find it easier to pray and to think of God as a reality than others do, so men and women of excellent character and good minds differ in intensity of interest and in manner of expression upon this theme which some have called the most important subject that can engage the thought of man.

Every discerning pastor knows this difference of attitude in his own congregation and among some of its best minds. For instance, I know a grand Christian character who is one of the most loyal churchmen of my acquaintance. Once after hearing his pastor preach a strong sermon on immortality, full of assurance and conviction, this gentleman remarked to me: "I would give everything I possess to believe all that my pastor believes on the subject of life everlasting." And I number among my friends a royal personage of ebullient spirit whose churchmanship on the whole suffers when compared with that of the friend just alluded to who has said more than once in my hearing, "There are some things in the Christian doctrine I cannot fully accept, but I believe fully and without any reservation that life goes on after death." And thus it goes. The human mind is not and cannot be standardized on any subject, even though it wants to believe.

In this volume there is the same variegated pattern of high hills and low-lying valleys, mountain ranges and plateaus of thought on the subject of immortality. For example, Pericles, the eloquent Greek, urges those who hear him to find consolation in the reflection of deeds well done which will win for them an earthly immortality. The high-minded Seneca, who flourished in the early Christian era but seems never to have had any contact with Christians, begins a moral epistle with this sentence: "That day which you fear as being the end of all things is the birthday of your eternity." Sir Thomas Browne, who lived through the period of the Civil Wars in England, in the excerpt quoted, says: "There is nothing strictly immortal but immortality." The saintly Henry Vaughan coins the exquisite phrase, "Bright shoots of everlastingness." On the other hand, old Dr. Johnson, one of the most devout Christians who ever lived, was reconciled to the thought of death only after an heroic struggle. He was never disposed to regard the subject with complacency, but when death came, he met it as a Christian warrior should.

Curiously, Theodore Parker, a theological radical of his day and a bold crusader, is represented by a sermon in this book in which he celebrates an unshakable faith in immortality, affirms that he feels conscious of it, goes on to say that no miracle could make him more sure, not if "the sheeted dead burst cerement and shroud," rose before him assuring him that they lived and that he also should live again. To such, Dr. Parker avers he would say, "I knew all this before, why waste your heavenly speech?" Here, too, is the scientist, Sir Oliver Lodge, who, in

ponderous paragraphs, gives a reason for the belief that humanity is destined to live forever and forever. And so on and on;
bright lights and somber shadows; tentative, cautious conjec-
tures; affirmative, reassuring statements; vague dreams and
emphatic affirmations—so goes the adventure of *The Farther
Shore!*

III

A third thing that impresses me about this book, *The Farther
Shore,* is the amazing contrast between the Christian witness
to immortality and that of others represented in this notable
volume. Not quite midway in this book, with the "Moral
Essays" of Seneca on one side and the "Meditations" of Marcus
Aurelius on the other, are the quotations from the Bible. A
little more than seven pages are devoted to the Christian Scriptures. The change of tone is not only striking, it is astonishing.
The music, if we might think of this anthology as a symphony,
passes from minor to major, with no intermission; and such
music! It is no longer plaintive but *fortissimo.* The mellow flute
is laid aside for the strident trumpet. The muted cello gives
place to the high-sounding cymbals. Or, to vary the figure, night
with a few large stars and a pale moon gives place to a rosy
dawn that suffuses the eastern skies with a golden glow. It is
daybreak everywhere. It is the White Morning!

And on that White Morning there was a tomb in a garden,
and that tomb was *empty,* and the great gray stone that was
placed against it had been rolled away, and a young man in
that tomb said to the women that had come early with spices
that they might anoint the body of Jesus: "Be not affrighted,
you seek Jesus of Nazareth, which was crucified: He is risen;
he is not here: behold the place where they laid him." That
empty tomb in the garden of Joseph of Arimathea is the most
eloquent fact in this anthology; and, for that matter, in the
Bible itself. For, from that empty tomb there emerged the

Church of Christ. Inspired by that tenantless tomb, in grand procession there came host upon host of Jesus' disciples to turn the world upside down and to give their lives freely for His dear sake.

On this Easter Sunday in the year of our Lord 1939, I turn to that one Clarion Voice which speaks upon this subject without hesitancy or doubt. He knows and knows that He knows. Listen, O fellow mortals, listen to the words of Jesus Christ:

Because I live, ye shall live also. . . . In my Father's house are many apartments; if it were not so I would have told you; I go to prepare a place for you. . . . I am the resurrection and the life. . . . Whoever has seen me has seen the Father. . . . This day shalt thou be with me in paradise.

And St. Paul avers with stouthearted enthusiasm:

For this corruptible must put on incorruption, and this mortal must put on immortality. So when this corruptible shall have put on incorruption, and this mortal shall have put on immortality, then shall be brought to pass the saying that is written, Death is swallowed up in victory. O death, where is thy sting? O grave, where is thy victory? The sting of death is sin; and the strength of sin is the law. But thanks be to God, which giveth us the victory through our Lord Jesus Christ. Therefore, my beloved brethren, be ye stedfast, unmoveable, always abounding in the work of the Lord, forasmuch as ye know that your labor is not in vain in the Lord [ASV].

Also, St. John is very bold and says:

And I saw a new heaven and a new earth: for the first heaven and the first earth were passed away; and there was no more sea. And I John saw the holy city, new Jerusalem, coming down from God out of heaven, prepared as a bride adorned for her husband. And I heard a great voice out of heaven saying, Behold, the tabernacle of God is with men, and he will dwell with them, and they shall be his people, and God himself shall be with them, and be their God. And God shall wipe away all tears from their eyes; and there shall be no more death, neither sorrow, nor crying, neither shall there be any more pain: for the former things are passed away. And he that sat upon the throne said, Behold, I make all things new. And he said unto me, Write: for these words are true and faithful. And he said unto me, It is done. I am Alpha and Omega, the beginning and the end. I will give unto him that is athirst of the fountain of the water of life freely. He that overcometh shall inherit all things; and I will be his God, and he shall be my son.

These words from Jesus, St. Paul and St. John have been tried and tested for nineteen hundred years; they have been weighed in the balance and found not wanting; upon the lips of ten thousand times ten thousand, they have been appraised, approved, put to the acid test. O Hallelujah Chorus, sing on!

IV

The title of this book fascinates me—*The Farther Shore*. The figure of a sea as a symbol of death is very old, but it is still effective. On this side is life, bordered by the nearer shore; and yonder is the farther shore; and between that shore and this is the Great Sea. The poets love to refer to death as a sea, and those of us who go out upon it as voyagers upon a cruise of discovery.

In this connection I recall an incident which happened some years ago, but the recollection is ever so vivid today. In company with a very dear kinsman, who was more like an elder brother than an uncle, I stood on the sand dunes at Cape Henry, where the waters of Chesapeake Bay widen and deepen as they merge with the Atlantic Ocean. It was a gray, bleak day in middle autumn, the sun obscured by low-hanging clouds and a fine mist falling. Back of us was a swamp, surrounded by a tangle of underbrush from which the wild notes of a bird I could not identify rose and fell in melancholy cadence. Off the ocean shore, a quarter of a mile distant, a bell buoy clanged its warning signal at regular intervals.

As we stood on the sand dunes that somber afternoon and looked about us a small schooner moved proudly down the bay and turned her prow toward the misty deep. Wordlessly we watched the little vessel until she merged with the misty distance and was lost to our view; then I spoke: "What an adventure! So small a ship, so great an ocean!" "No, not as much of an adventure as you think," replied my uncle. "You see, the ocean is charted, there's a navigator on board and a pilot. The strong likelihood is that that ship will reach her port, despite thick weather, storms and rough waves." And being a preacher, I tucked the episode in some corner of my mind, and today I feel like saying to the Author of life, "Thanks for the memory."

For, more than anyone else who ever lived, Jesus charted this life and the other life for us; and He is the Pilot whom we hope to see when we "have crossed the bar." He was and is the Master of Life, as well as the Way and the Truth. He knows and knows that He knows. He spoke the last word on this subject of immortality.

The farther shore is nearer to us than we have thought. Eternal Life begins *here*. Living the immortal life *now* is the duty and the privilege of all God's children. The old camp-meeting hymn "I'm Living in Canaan Now" is not as fanciful as we once judged it might be. Hearken to John, the seraphic: "Beloved, now we are sons of God, and it is not yet made manifest what we shall be." The "farther shore" is not so far after all. It is very, very close; closer than we think.

Musing on this solemn figure of the sea and of the farther shore, reflecting on the last voyage into the unknown, these words from Lyman Abbott are singularly appropriate:

I look forward to the Great Adventure, which now cannot be far off, with awe, but not with apprehension. I enjoy my work, my home, my friends, my life. I shall be sorry to part with them. But always I have stood in the bow looking forward with hopeful anticipation to the life before me. When the time comes for my embarkation, and the ropes are cast off and I put out to sea, I think I shall still be standing in the bow, and still looking forward with eager curiosity and glad hopefulness to the new world to which the unknown voyage will bring me.

Someday, we know not when, we, too, shall be standing in the bow unafraid, and at the helm—the Pilot!

6

If I Sat Where They Sit

Then I came to them of the captivity at Tel-abib, that dwelt by
the river of Chebar, and I sat where they sat, and remained there
astonished among them seven days.   EZEKIEL 3:15

THE prophet Ezekiel, whose hard lot it was to serve his
exiled fellow countrymen in Babylonian captivity, was
greatly embittered when he first saw their plight. But he tells
us that when he "sat where they sat" he underwent a change of
heart and entered into a sympathetic understanding of what
they were undergoing.

This experience of the prophet says something to me as I
look back on a twenty-six-year pastorate in Detroit. For most of
these years I sat in the preacher's seat which, for a decade or
more, had been a high-backed, massive chair with ecclesiastical
symbols carved thereon. From that vantage point I looked out
over a congregation assembled to worship God, seventy per cent
of which represented the beloved flock I shepherded all too
inadequately.

I often wonder, were I able to take my five decades of experience as preacher-pastor back to the pew as a layman, what use
I would make of my observations from the occupancy of the
preacher's chair. I venture to chronicle here some of my reflec-
tions on this subject, speculating on what I would do if I sat
where they sit.

I

For one thing, I am sure I should sit well up toward the front
of the church. Pity the plight of the poor usher who courteously
conducts his quarry up the long center aisle, stops before a front

pew, steps aside to bow them in, only to discover they have helped themselves to seats a dozen rows back. It is a disconcerting experience for him and an unending occasion for amusement on the part of some of the congregation who find it diverting.

I have long been puzzled by the reluctance of so many church members to occupy the front seats in the house of God. Is it due to the notion that to sit in the front of a church may seem to put one's piety on parade? It may be. Do the words of Jesus expressing disapproval of those who loved the front seats in the synagogue help explain this reluctance? Perhaps. Is the possibility of being unexpectedly called upon by the minister, say, to lower a window or substitute as a deacon to take an offering, also in the picture? It may be so. I do not for a moment believe that faithful churchmen object to serving in such a capacity, but I can understand and sympathize with their dislike of being catapulted into activities of this sort on short notice and in the presence of the congregation. Doubtless there are other reasons. Not everyone is so frank as that gentleman who once confided to me that he habitually took a back seat so as to make a quick exit following the benediction. Perhaps he had something there.

Personally, I enjoy a front seat at church or any kind of public meeting on several counts: I like to watch the play of emotion on the speaker's face. Then, too, by sitting well up toward the front in a service of worship I am not distracted by the many movements and slight confusions incidental to the gathering of a congregation, and so find it easier to acquire the meditative mood. It is not, perhaps, a serious matter, this preponderance of rear-seat worshipers, but I strongly favor, as a congregational policy, the seating of a church from the front to the back, not from the rear to the front. When I sit where they sit, I shall continue to ask to be shown to a front seat, not solely because I enjoy sitting there but also that I may set a good example which I hope will be followed by others.

If I sat where they sit, I should plan to reach the sanctuary at least ten minutes before the opening of the services. This would enable me to be seated well up in front, with a period of meditation to prepare me for the worship of God. I should prefer not to talk to anyone at such a time, although I am a sociable being and like to meet and converse with all sorts and conditions of men, women and little children.

The ten minutes before the opening of a church service are precious and can be employed fruitfully, sitting quietly there. It is good to think on God, on prayer, on Jesus Christ and the power of His endless life. Then, there is the organ prelude to be enjoyed. I love organ music, and with a master of the keyboard in charge, the deep, majestic notes lift me to exalted moods. If I came into the worship after the opening prayer, or missed the reading of the Scriptures, I should feel I had lost the clue to the theme of the sermon and be obliged to discover it as best I could, thereby being the loser because of my tardy appearance at worship in the house of God.

In 1910 I heard Reginald John Campbell, then at the peak of his fame, preach in City Temple, London. He was under fire at that time from conservative quarters due to his book *The New Theology,* which but lately had been published. I got to the Temple a full hour before the meeting was to begin, yet long lines of people were waiting for the doors to open. I worked my way close to the entrance, and when the doors were unlocked and flung ajar, the push of the throng carried me well into the spacious sanctuary. Spying a vacant seat close to the front I managed to reach it, and sat down.

I looked about me. The choir loft . . . the great marble pulpit . . . the ornate lectern. Yes, I mused, Joseph Parker once stood in that pulpit and thundered against wrongdoing, in both low and high places. Prime ministers, peers of the realm, and General William Booth spoke from that pulpit. . . . Suddenly the lights flared up and the choir and preacher entered. A hush fell over the people. Dr. Campbell stood up to pray, his hair, prematurely gray, crowning a serenely beautiful face. And the sermon was on that beatific text, "I shall be satisfied, when I awake, with thy likeness."

What went on behind me for the next hour I cannot say, but what happened in front of me I saw, and heard and felt, to my everlasting good. My brethren, write me down as one who chooses to arrive at the church service ahead of time and loves unashamedly the front seats in the house of the Lord.

The grand lines of John Milton from "Il Penseroso" come to mind—lines which express fully and gloriously what my imperfect speech and pen have not been able to frame, save in part, and feebly:

> But let my due feet never fail
> To walk the studious cloister's pale,
> And love the high embowèd roof,
> With antique pillars massy proof,
> And storied windows richly dight,
> Casting a dim religious light.
> There let the pealing organ blow,
> To the full-voiced quire below,
> In service high and anthems clear,
> As may with sweetness, through mine ear,
> Dissolve me into ecstasies,
> And bring all Heaven before mine eyes.

II

If I sat where they sit, I should want to put on the collection plate a weekly offering which in some real sense represented me. I should feel cheap and lacking something fundamentally Christian if I treated the collection plate shabbily. When I was a very young parson and in my first pastorate, I received into membership a girl from a Catholic church. Shortly thereafter, her mother asked me how much her daughter ought to pay toward the support of our church. Being young and inexperienced, I treated the question as of secondary importance and with an expansive gesture disposed of the inquiry by saying, "Oh, there is no great hurry about that. It is for you to decide at your leisure." The mother replied, "Well, all I've got to say is that it is a lot cheaper to belong to your church than to the Catholic Church."

At the time, I took this as a compliment. I know better now. The reflection was on me. I should have said to that mother: "Give all you can afford. The ancient Jews gave a tenth, can a Christian conscientiously give less?" But I didn't know any better. I had not yet learned the dignity and righteousness of the stewardship of life and possessions. If I sat where they sit, I should hope that my preacher would talk of the necessity and nobility of monetary gifts to the Lord, as the Spirit moved him, and make no apology for so doing.

While I am on this subject, let me remark that the word "steward" as used in the New Testament is an archaic term. Personally, I prefer the word "trustee." The steward of the lands of the Bible was an overseer and a trusted servant, responsible for the property over which he had control or supervision. Naturally, he was obliged to give from time to time an accounting of his stewardship. We are all stewards or trustees of life, property, personality, influence. God is the owner, and we are accountable for our trusteeship of that which belongs to another. Wealth is a social product and should serve society. The use we make of property or other possessions has a social effect, either good or evil.

In one of my earliest pastorates, sitting where you sit was a construction engineer who faithfully set apart a tenth of his income to be distributed in what he called "the Lord's work." He was a highly educated man, a lover of music, an entertaining personality. One memorable day this man came to me and asked if there was any place in the church where a hundred dollars could be used advantageously. Imagine a question like that! As if there was any church anywhere that didn't have a half dozen uses for a hundred dollars which seemed to drop from the skies,

I assured the donor that I knew exactly where that gift would come as an answer to prayer, and I thanked him ardently. He went on to explain to me that this hundred dollars was part of his tithe money, that he had set it aside for some specific cause, only to discover that the need in that particular place had already been supplied. The money was returned to him, but he regarded it not as his own and would not think of spending it on himself. Thus he brought it to me, and I have never ceased to recall the event, for it made an indelible impression upon me.

The shortest sermon ever preached of which we have any record was on this subject of stewardship. The famous Jonathan Swift, the able but acidulous dean of St. Patrick's Cathedral, Dublin, one day made a public appeal for some needy cause. He announced as his text, "He that giveth to the poor lendeth to the Lord." He said: "If you like the security, plank down the gold." That was all. That was enough. If I sat where they sit, I should want to give a good account of my Christian trusteeship.

III

If I sat where they sit, I should feel elated and eagerly expectant as the minister stood up to preach. Here is a man about to bring forth treasures new and old from the unfailing resources of the Faith: the Holy Scriptures, the noblest of literature, the best of his reading and the fruits of lonely contemplation on his theme, commingled with much journeying along the mystic pathway of prayer.

If the sermon was excellent, or if it stirred me deeply and made me feel the Unseen Presence of the Eternal, I should not fail to tell the preacher so, and thank him for a giant half hour. If I found it difficult to see him after the service, it would give me pleasure to write him the next day or maybe telephone him Sunday night, say, about 9:45 or 10:00 o'clock, thus possibly contributing something toward a good night's sleep for my dominie.

If the sermon was below the preacher's best, because of

physical condition or a week of organizational exactions and church finance anxieties, my attentiveness would be, if anything, more sympathetic than usual. Always I should want to assume that his falling below the high level of sermonic excellence was not due to carelessness on my preacher's part, for I could scarcely conceive of his failing to regard every sermon as demanding his utmost, that he would not rely on the occasion for an inspiration that best comes from the hardest kind of work. Poor preaching due to lack of preparation is inexcusable.

As a dominie who loves both his vocation and the national game, it occurs to me that a relief preacher would be just the thing when the regular pulpiteer is groggy, shows signs of wildness, and the congregation becomes restless and sleepy.

A tense and often dramatic period in a closely-contested ball game is when a relief pitcher comes in at a critical juncture. The starting pitcher, after several successful innings having slowed down or lost control, is waved out of the box, and a fresh twirler takes his place. Sometimes it works and sometimes it doesn't, but it is good baseball.

Imagine how quickly the people would come to life as one of the office-bearers waves the fading parson from the pulpit and signals a fresh preacher to take his place. The innovation has much to commend it. For instance, it might stimulate church attendance, since there would be no prolongation of a poor sermon, and a fresh voice would always be on tap.

It would mean, of course, some additional expense to keep a couple of parsons "warming up" every Sunday, going over their sermons so as to be ready to go into action on a moment's notice. But it would be worth all it cost. Then, too, it might act favorably on the regular preacher, put him on his toes, inspire him to be well up in his sermonic stuff. Being waved out of the pulpit to metaphorical showers wouldn't be exactly an enjoyable experience.

Still again, such an innovation might work wonders with church officials. It would give them new responsibilities. The office-bearer vested with the authority to change preachers would have to be on his job and obliged to watch his minister closely for signs of weakening. His office would take on an additional importance, and instead of a paucity of candidates as has often been the case, there would be a scramble for offices that once went begging.

The more I think of it, the more the idea of a relief preacher to preach in pinches grows on me. It has a lot to commend it; and the bare possibility of some churches trying it out might work such a miracle in the mind of the clergy as to make the experiment wholly unnecessary.

In a more serious vein, if I sat where they sit, I should not expect to be in agreement always with my preacher's pulpit utterances. Indeed, if such were the case, I should be troubled about him and about myself. I should of course expect him to have a firm and intelligent grasp on the real essentials of the Christian gospel—I mean a sturdy belief that God is and that He is a rewarder of them that seek Him; an unending and increasing loyalty to the Spirit and Saviourhood of Jesus Christ; and an unshaken conviction that humanity with all its frailties is worth all the sacrificial pangs that a redemptive and healing ministry demands.

However, I should find it refreshing if my preacher were unafraid of plowing fresh furrows in fields that have been gone over myriad times and have seen numerous seasons of seedtime and harvest come and go. I would even welcome some of my pet theories being subjected to his pulpit scrutiny and my favorite and long-accepted beliefs being flooded with a new and mellow radiance. For one of the wonderments of the gospel is the fact that after twenty centuries it can be presented in a new dress and continue to charm and challenge.

IV

If I sat where they sit, I know I should wish to greet any stranger seated near me, when the period of worship came to an end. In some of our larger city churches this is a sadly neglected courtesy. There may be explanations that place this strange neglect in a better light but I have never heard one that satisfied me.

I recall just one churchman in all the years I have been in the ministry who told me he did not want anybody at church to speak to him, nor did he wish to speak to anybody. "I come to church to worship God," he declared, "not to be pawed over or to paw over anybody else." This is a novel viewpoint, but I think this man spoke for himself, and very few others. Almost everybody welcomes a greeting in a church and especially so if he be a newcomer in a strange community. The story will be recalled of the little girl who, returning from church, was asked the text of the sermon. She knitted her brows and thought hard, then replied: "I think it was 'Many were cold but few were frozen.'" And I have had many a good laugh over the story told about the famous Admiral Robley D. Evans who, worshiping in a city church where they had the pew rental system, slipped into a vacant seat and bowed his head in prayer. Looking up and about him, he observed the man seated next to him was regarding him in an unfriendly fashion. Shortly he pushed a note toward the rugged old sea dog, who opened it and read: "I pay $3,000 for this pew." The Admiral made a notation on the slip of paper and returned it to the pewholder. What he had written was this: "You pay too —— much." I leave the adjective to your imagination.

The house of God should be a friendly place, made so by the spirit of good will and brotherhood mediated through the consecrated personalities of the congregation. The welcome need not be lusty or loud; it should be warm, brotherly and radiantly sincere.

If I sat where they sit, I could not be content until I found some responsibilities to shoulder in connection with the life of the congregation. If a men's club was in the picture, I should wish to be a part of it; if it should happen that I was appointed to a committee or elected as a member of the official group, I would feel honor-bound to accept the responsibility and regard it as a distinction not to be lightly esteemed. Somewhere Dr. Fosdick has said that worship at the church is not "the service"; that the service begins after the worshiper leaves the church.

Just as in the Congress of the United States, the main business is done not on the floor of the public assembly, important as that is, but in the labor that goes on in the committee rooms, so in a measure is the business, social and administrative life of a church done in and through the organizations, societies and guilds. Participation in these groups widens one's acquaintance among the membership and expands his conception of the church's world mission. It would be a mistake, however, to set these two functions of church membership one over against the other. They are the two sides of the shield—worship and work, preaching and practice. Moreover, the area of Christian living is as boundless as one's life contacts and relationships.

Experience and observation go to prove that the more faithful people are in attendance upon public worship the more usable they are in the organizations of the church, and what is perhaps still more to the point, the more they are willing to be used. Church membership means not any one privilege, duty or responsibility, but all of these; it is a world within a world, a family, a little bit of heaven come down to earth.

If I sat where they sit, I can think of several other things I should hope to do or not to do. Yet the longer I reflect on the subject, the more I find myself wondering if I could give a better account of my churchmanship than have the faithful men, women and children on whose dear faces my gaze has often rested through the fleeting years. Something tells me that I should do pretty much as they have done, most likely not nearly as well. God love the vast unheralded host of men, women, and little children too, who sit through the services of the churches; God love them much, for without their inspiring presence no sermon of redemptive power could be preached. Hail to the brightness of Zion's glad morning, for we sit together in a heavenly place!

7

The Fellowship of the Unashamed

For I am not ashamed of the gospel of Christ: for it is the power of God unto salvation to every one that believeth; to the Jew first, and also to the Greek.   ROMANS 1:16

Stand fast therefore in the liberty wherewith Christ hath made us free, and be not entangled again with the yoke of bondage.

GALATIANS 5:1

If the Alps piled in cold and silence be the emblem of despotism, we joyfully take the ever restless ocean for ours, only pure because never still.   WENDELL PHILLIPS
Phi Beta Kappa oration
Harvard, 1881

THE first and second of these statements are from the mind and heart of one who had been an unashamed Jew, a man of culture and indomitable will, who gave himself and all he possessed to the furtherance of the gospel, which he had aforetime fiercely assailed. Once this man was converted to the Christian faith, his career of incredible activity began. He was a flaming evangelist, a founder of churches, a shepherd of souls, a polemicist of power, a writer of immortal letters, a much-traveled missionary of the cross. He died a martyr, this one-time rabbi, who became the apostle Paul, and, next to Jesus Christ himself, the greatest figure in the pages of the New Testament.

The third affirmation is an utterance of an unashamed American citizen, born to the purple, highly-placed and highly-trained, a superb orator, who turned his back on preferment, ease and comfort to become the champion of the poor, the lowly, the undone and the disinherited, Wendell Phillips of

Boston. A statue of this man stands on Boston Common, and in his hands is a broken chain, symbol of his liberating labors in behalf of the oppressed and the forgotten.

Professor Elton Trueblood in his powerful little book, *Foundations for Reconstruction,* holds that the real enemy of religion is not irreligion, but what he calls a "vague religiosity." The real enemy, he says, is not the Red organizer who openly opposes the Church, but the reputable citizen who adopts a patronizing attitude toward the Church by the gesture of joining it when he has no idea of genuine commitment to its gospel. "Our mild religiosity," Professor Trueblood continues, "will not only fail to support a sagging civilization, it cannot long retain itself. As the crisis advances we shall either become openly pagan or we shall be driven to leave this temporarily pleasant middle ground to the fourth alternative, that of commitment to the will of the living God in a radical Christianity that is not ashamed to be frankly missionary and evangelical." Professor Trueblood calls upon us for the creation of a Fellowship of the Unashamed, with the result that "Ours should then become one of those glorious ages of revival." But we are a long way from that now, he concedes.

The Fellowship of the Unashamed! Unashamed of familiarity with the Bible! Unashamed of the practice of prayer! Unashamed of rugged honesty! Unashamed of the missionary passion. Unashamed of the doctrine of a free Church in a free country! Unashamed of the ideals and principles and spirit of Him who came to bring us life, and that more abundantly!

I

We have every reason to be Unashamed of the Protestant Reformation, Unashamed of what it accomplished, Unashamed of its illustrious leader and of those associated with him in this stupendous task.

Luther was but thirty-three when on October 31, 1517, he nailed to the door of the Castle Church at Wittenberg his

Ninety-five Theses—the same age as Jefferson when he wrote the Declaration of Independence. He was a son of poverty and of privation. If it be true that not sparing the rod is the best way to save a child from being spoiled, Luther should be able to qualify as one of the great unspoiled of history. His peasant parents used corporal punishment plentifully. The boy knew nothing of ease or physical comforts. He was naturally religious, entered the priesthood against his father's wishes, who had hoped he would become a lawyer. Full of vitality and of boundless energy, his excellent tenor voice helped to pay his tuition. In his study of the Bible, a flaming text in Romans profoundly affected his life. The arresting words that quite startled him when first he saw their implications were these: "The just shall live by faith." The sale of indulgences by representatives of the Church touched the quick of his conscience, and he struck a blow for religious liberty that reverberated the world around. Excommunicated by the Pope, he burned the papal bull at nine o'clock on the 12th of December, 1520; and thus he broke with the most powerful organization of his day.

Professor Thomas N. Lindsay, in his *History of the Reformation*, states that Luther's message and movement were democratic in that they, (1) destroyed the aristocracy of the saints; (2) leveled the barriers between the layman and the priest; (3) taught the equality of all men before God, and (4) the right of every man of faith to stand in God's presence whatever be his rank and condition of life. Dr. Frederick D. Kershner in his *Pioneers of Christian Thought* words it a little differently, but the essence is the same. He holds that three principles stand out as basic in the teachings of Luther: first, his insistence on the Bible as the only authority in religion; second, the doctrine of justification by faith; and third, emphasis upon the right of private judgment in matters of religion.

This is not the time to enter into a detailed discussion or interpretation of these principles which became the cornerstone of Protestantism. Their implications are preached in myriad pulpits every Sunday in this and other nations. These principles have in them the heartbeat of rugged thinking. They call us to the preservation of freedoms that were purchased at so great a price—freedoms that stir our emotions like the steady beat of a drum or the strident notes of a bugle. Let it be granted that we do not always live up to these principles. Let it be confessed that we handle some of them a little gingerly, as for instance the right of private interpretation of the Scriptures. Let it be acknowledged that we have not given these fundamental principles the fullest application. Yet withal, we live and breathe the air, both religiously and politically, that was purified by the thought and deeds of the great German reformer. Credit too should go to John Wycliffe, "The Morning Star of the Reformation," to John Huss, John Calvin and John Knox.

Something should be said, even if but briefly, of those who were most closely associated with Luther in the reforms he inaugurated; for instance, Philipp Melanchthon, who was Luther's shadow. He was a much gentler soul than his chief, more lovable and gracious. Melanchthon was to Luther what John the beloved disciple must have been to Simon Peter. Also worthy of mention is Huldreich Zwingli, the Swiss reformer. He and Luther did not always agree. The Swiss was more liberal than the German, less mystical perhaps and more practical. Their difference over the Lord's Supper is a historic episode full of color. The issue was realistic, and there are many of us who would say that Zwingli had the better of the argument. Nor should we overlook Erasmus, held by some to be the foremost scholar of all time. Nearly everybody was serious in those faraway times and particularly so in the realm of religion; dreadfully, terribly serious, and perhaps there was a reason. Erasmus had a sense of humor, an eye for the comic and an appreciation of it, even when the spirit of controversy hung like a pall over classroom and church. Some of the biographers of the Reformation period criticize Erasmus and call him a trimmer. A brilliant American lecturer, who was good at coining epigrams, said of

Erasmus that he spent his life trying to tread on eggshells without breaking them. This is clever rhetoric, but not wholly true. Erasmus was among the few of the reformers who saw how far Luther's movement would go. He, too, wished to reform the Church and go back to the simplicity and spiritual power of the New Testament Church; but he foresaw the schism, the divisions that were certain to follow, and so he drew back and did not go all the way with Luther. Nevertheless, he made his contribution, and deserves honorable mention.

Luther had his limitations, as have all men. We have to take our great men as we find them. We have to remember the times in which they lived and the conditions under which they wrought. Sometimes it is necessary to take the mantle of charity and walk backward and cover the nakedness of their errors and the splotches that stained their escutcheon. History is incurious as to the faults and foibles of great men, providing they made an enduring deposit of substantial achievements for the betterment of humanity. Luther had little sympathy with the working class. He failed to give his support to the Peasants' War. Sometimes he threw wild words around recklessly. Theologically he was an Augustinian, and an enemy of the doctrine of free will. But these are like spots on the sun. They do not detract from his essential greatness, and they show how human he was, even as you and I. Luther has been called "a practical mystic." That he was sometimes impractical is admitted, but the lusty German always struck hard for what he believed to be right. He stands out on the skyline of history, a titanic figure, involved in numerous controversies but never failing in his belief that "A Mighty Fortress is our God."

We are unashamed of the mighty Reformation which emerged from Martin Luther's heroic leadership, but we are sometimes ashamed of the manner and spirit in which the principles of Protestantism are presented. The poet Tennyson once said that in religion one has to choose between bigotry on the one hand and flabbiness on the other. Not many will agree with this position. For one, I repudiate it. I hold that there is a halfway house where one can stand loyally by his convictions and be neither bigoted nor flabby. I think this halfway house is where Protestantism should establish residence.

Nothing good is gained by calling names and imputing ulterior motives, either in religion or politics. An American citizen is at his best and highest when he stands squarely on his religious principles and votes his political convictions without stooping to impugn motives or indulge in the bitter language of hate. The word "protestant" comes from two Latin words meaning "to be a witness"; and I agree with a noble fellow Protestant that the major role of Protestantism is to witness to Christian truth and the mind and spirit of Jesus Christ.

Protestantism is a movement for freedom both in government and in Church. Protestantism is an invitation to think for oneself; and among other obligations resting on us is that of thinking no evil and always speaking what we hold to be the truth in the spirit of good will and love. My authority for this statement is none other than the greatest of the apostles, St. Paul!

When we think of this Reformation which shook the world we recall how admirably it illustrates Wendell Phillips' scintillating epigram, "If the Alps piled in cold and silence be the emblem of despotism, we joyously take the ever restless ocean for ours, only pure because never still."

II

We are Unashamed of the heritage of freedom which has come down to us from the Founding Fathers of our beloved America; Unashamed of the Constitution into which fifty-five men, selected because of their standing and ability, poured the plenitude of their minds and hearts; Unashamed of the Bill of Rights, which is the soul of that historic document.

These fifty-five men deserve our praise and lasting gratitude. It is interesting to know that twenty-nine of them were graduates of colleges or universities. Of the fifty-five, thirty-five were lawyers or had studied law; eight were merchants; six were farmers; three, physicians; two, ministers of the gospel; and one, a printer. These men spent a long, hot summer in Philadelphia, beating out the metal of the instrument upon which our government rests. For weeks they seemed hopelessly divided, and at such a time Benjamin Franklin made a motion that they send out in the city for a clergyman to come into their assembly and ask guidance of Almighty God that they might complete their important task. Colonel Alexander Hamilton opposed the motion, but he was careful to explain that he had no objection to prayer being offered, but that he feared if word got out (they were meeting behind locked doors) that the delegates were in such a pickle that they were obliged to send for a clergyman to pray them out of it, the people might lose confidence in their ability to do the high business of the hour. It would seem that the motion was lost, but we may believe that every one of the fifty-five men prayed to God for guidance and for wisdom. Their prayers were answered, for many years later William E. Gladstone was to say of the American Constitution that it was the most inspired document struck off by the mind of man at a given time.

I have said that the soul of the Constitution is the Bill of Rights, which is contained in the first ten Amendments, and made law December 15, 1791. This Bill of Rights protects the citizen from his government, and avers that there are some things that the government cannot do, and among these, no interference in the exercise of religion, free speech, popular assembly and the right of petition. There are other freedoms involved in this Bill of Rights, but these four are basic. Not only is this a Bill of Rights, it is a Bill of Duties. We talk too much about our rights, and too little about our duties. It should be noted that our American democracy, system of government, Constitution, Bill of Rights—all of these are related to the Protestant Reformation led by Martin Luther. Indeed, an American church historian of high standing, Dr. Frederick D. Kershner, says that in both America and England, the principles of the Reformation have found expression in religion and politics alike. He is of the opinion that these principles would not have achieved any place in politics if they had not first found embodiment in religion. He goes further. He says, "Martin Luther rather than Oliver Cromwell or George Washington was the author of modern political freedom." This statement may be debatable, but there is truth in it.

The weaknesses of a democracy and of Protestantism are the same, namely, the abuse of liberty and inefficiency. It is not possible to have free speech, free exercise of religion and a free press, without differences of opinion, clashes and cleavages over issues both theological and political. But it is better to have these, with sometimes their annoyances and embarrassments, than to be held together in a viselike grip by a dictator or a tyrant. There is much to be said for the privilege of making our own mistakes, and the best cure for the ills of a democracy is more democracy.

Fisher Ames, one of the Founding Fathers, said a striking thing more than a century and a half ago. "A monarchy," he declared, "is like a warship, strong and proud, but any hidden rock may sink her; while a democracy is like a raft, hard to steer, and your feet are always wet, but thank God, nothing can sink her." Brilliant rhetoric? Undoubtedly, but not wholly true. No matter what form of government men are under, the human passions are the same. A democracy is subject to the same frailties, stupidity, corruption, lawlessness, as is any other kind of government. The saving salt of a democracy, however, is that the people themselves have the power to correct their mistakes. Never is it possible to have a new and better world without new and better human beings.

The deadliest enemies of our institutions are not outside, but within our borders: complacency, neglect of the ballot, indifference to the kind of men selected for public office, the lowering of standards of morality, corruption in high and low places. We are unashamed of the heritage of our Founding Fathers, but we are ashamed of an undiscerning and ungrateful citizenship that forgets that "Eternal vigilance is the price of liberty."

According to the Constitution of the United States this is not a Protestant nation, nor a Catholic nation, nor a Jewish nation—but a nation where Protestants, Catholics and Jews are given the right of the free exercise of religion, with Church and State forever separate! This is basic Americanism, and woe unto us and our freedom if we tamper with the Bill of Rights, juggle its letter or repudiate its spirit. Can you not see wisdom and justice in this position? Surely you can if you think back and recall certain horrible segments of history. Our Founding Fathers remembered vividly what happened in Europe and other continents when Protestants were persecuted because they were *Protestants,* Catholics were persecuted because they were *Catholics,* and Jews were persecuted because they were *Jews,* and they were determined that that should not happen here, so they gave us the Bill of Rights. Again I quote Wendell Phillips' pertinent epigram, "If the Alps piled in cold and silence be the emblem of despotism, we joyously take the ever restless ocean for ours, only pure because never still."

III

We are Unashamed of the experiments in co-operative Christianity looking to a closer unity and a spiritual solidarity such as Protestantism has yet to achieve, so we thank God and take fresh courage.

Surely we are not unaware of the progress made toward the reunion of the divided House of God in our Protestant world within the last quarter of a century. That progress is encouraging. In 1929 the union between two great Presbyterian bodies in Scotland took place, resulting in the Church of Scotland, with a membership of some 1,300,000. But before this merger occurred there had been other important if less spectacular unions among Scottish Presbyterians. In 1932 the three Methodist bodies in Great Britain were united without a dissenting vote. In France, where Protestantism is weak, numbering about a million, and split four ways, a reunion has come about. In Canada, the union of the Methodists, Congregationalists and about seventy per cent of the Presbyterians, resulting in the United Church of Canada, was an achievement of magnitude, an expression of statesmanship of a noble spiritual quality. The union of three bodies of Methodism in America is a victory of wide significance. Eight million Methodists cannot be wrong on this issue as the souls of John Wesley, George Whitefield and a host of others march grandly on.

In the decade from 1926 to 1936 no less than 53 definite approaches toward church union were undertaken in various parts of the world. Fifteen resulted in full and final unions. The World Church is now a going concern in which some 44 nations are represented and 151 church bodies have taken membership. (These figures refer to the time when this address was being prepared.) Mr. John D. Rockefeller, Jr., never made a wiser contribution of his great wealth than the million dollars he gave to the World Council. If it is possible to make too much of this moving out toward a World Church, it is certainly possible to make too little of it. The service it rendered to a war-scourged Europe drenched in sadness, of a nature spiritual and moral as well as physical, is too great to be adequately asssessed.

I was brought up in a little town in northeastern Missouri with a population of less than a thousand, and five churches. Now, every church had a bell in those days, and you could tell the denomination by the tone of the bell. On Sunday morning the Presbyterian bell would begin to ring (it had a mellow tone) and seemed to say: "Come and worship here! Come and worship here!" Then the Southern Methodist bell joined the Presbyterian bell (it had a metallic sound) and it said: "O come and pray with us! O come and pray with us!" Then the

Baptist bell swung into action. The Baptist Church was the largest in town and had the biggest bell. It boomed out "Here's the place to come! Here's the place to come!" Next the Methodist Episcopal Church, located in the northwest part of the town, chimed in. That church was the weakest in numbers and worldly possessions. Some of our saints were in that church, and the bell had a kind of mournful note and seemed to say: "O don't forget us! O don't forget us!" Then my own, the Christian Church bell, joined the chorus and rang out clear and strong, saying: "Come and hear the truth! Come and hear the truth!"

O those ringing church bells of the long ago! I seem to hear them ringing now. Even as a little boy I was puzzled because of our community divisions in Christianity on Sundays, prayer-meeting nights and during revivalistic meetings. Is it any better today in my old home town? In the spirit of Christian co-operation, yes. There is but one Methodist Church there now, yet there are four congregations struggling, where one strong church could say to the community for religion, what the large consolidated high school says to the community in behalf of unity in the realm of education.

The glorious Head of the Church prayed for the oneness of all those who believe on Him, and we must not forget that these believers are in every communion of Christendom, from the smallest and the humblest, to the most populous and the most powerful. Perhaps we have been thinking too much of the churches and too little about *the* Church. At one of the plenary sessions at the Oxford Conference in 1937, a brief speech was made by an American delegate, who said, "We came here talking about *our* churches; we are going back home to talk about *the* Church." And yet, paradoxical as it may seem, though *the* Church is greater than the churches, *the* Church draws its substance, its vitality and its power from the churches. More and more our church life must be a community of interests. I mean now the life of our congregations, which we

love to think of as families of the Christ. Notice this word
"community." It means to come together bringing gifts, not
necessarily money, but gifts of mind and heart, the spirit of
forgiveness, the passion for justice, a genius for good will. I
think we do well to pray with the poet Whittier:

> Forgive, O Lord, our severing ways,
> The rival altars that we raise,
> The wrangling tongues that mar thy praise!
>
> Thy grace impart! In time to be
> Shall one great temple rise to Thee—
> Thy Church our broad humanity.
>
> White flowers of love its walls shall climb,
> Soft bells of peace shall ring its chime,
> Its days shall all be holy time.
>
> A sweeter song shall then be heard,
> Confessing, in a world's accord,
> The inward Christ, the living Word.
>
> That song shall swell from shore to shore.
> One hope, one faith, one love restore
> The seamless robe that Jesus wore.

I aver that as we review the history of the Protestant Reformation we are unashamed of what it was and what it did. We
are unashamed of its leaders. But we are ashamed of our
failure to live up to the principles and the spirit of a movement
which has given us almost everything we prize. We are unashamed of the experiments and the progress looking to the
reunion of the divided house of God, although we are abashed
by our failure not to have done more. We are ashamed and
embarrassed that we have not gotten farther along the road to
unity and thus helped to answer the prayer of our Lord for the
oneness of His followers. We are unashamed of the heritage
left us by the Founding Fathers of our Republic, the Constitution and the Bill of Rights. But we acknowledge our shame
where the spirit and the letter of the Bill of Rights has been

flaunted and in some instances repudiated. We would repent and reconsecrate ourselves so that we could in all sincerity say with that unashamed Jew, "I am not ashamed of the gospel of Christ: for it is the power of God unto salvation to every one that believeth; to the Jew first, and also to the Greek." Likewise we would dedicate ourselves anew to the sentiment of that unashamed American citizen whose voice rang out at a critical hour with these words: "If the Alps piled in cold and silence be the emblem of despotism, we joyously take the ever restless ocean as ours, pure only because it is never still."

The Fellowship of the Unashamed: how we need to cherish and cultivate it! It was a vision of this victorious unnumbered host that caught the eye and held the gaze of John, the beloved disciple, in his lonely exile on the Isle of Patmos. You will recall the passage, for it is suffused in the White Light forever: "And one of the elders answered, saying unto me, These that are arrayed in the white robes, who are they, and whence came they? And I say unto him, My Lord, thou knowest. And he said to me, These are they that come out of the great tribulation, and they washed their robes, and made them white in the blood of the Lamb. . . . They shall hunger no more, neither thirst any more; neither shall the sun strike upon them, nor any heat . . . and God shall wipe away every tear from their eyes" (ASV).

> They healed sick hearts till theirs were broken
> They dried sad eyes till theirs lost sight
> We shall know at last by a certain token
> How they fought and fell in the fight.

The Fellowship of the Unashamed! Join up with it, work for it, sacrifice for it, live and die for it!

8

His Jerusalem and Ours

And it came to pass, when the time was come that he should be received up, he stedfastly set his face to go to Jerusalem.

LUKE 9:51

TO THIS day there is something sinister in the physical features of Jerusalem, capital of Palestine. For one thing, you are never out of sight of walls, grim and forbidding. You are constantly reminded by these ancient and battered ramparts of days when the city was embattled and under a devastating siege. The history of Jerusalem is written in blood, sweat and tears. It has been fought over fiercely and often. It has been the scene of deadly feuds waged by religious fanatics. On cloudy days the city is bleak and baleful, and when the hot noonday sun beats down upon Jerusalem, its lanes, to quote H. V. Morton, are "like a striped tiger."

To compare Jerusalem of Judea with Nazareth of Galilee, some ninety miles to the northwest, is like comparing a frowning fortress with a garden of flowers, a blazing desert with a fertile, well-watered plain.

In Jesus' day Jerusalem was a hotbed of political and religious strife; but for the faithful the city of the Great King had not lost its glory, and as the central place of worship, with the massive Temple rebuilt by Herod, attracted myriad worshipers. Under the Roman yoke at that period, the Jewish population for the most part made no effort to conceal their hatred of Roman rule. The governor of the province was Pontius Pilate, a proud pagan, who had no sympathy with the nationalistic fervor of his Jewish subjects, and no understanding of their devotion to the faith of their fathers. Pilate's way out of a critical situation was to wash his hands of the matter and call it a day.

I

Jesus was in Perea on the east side of Jordan when the incident occurred which supplies the text. His public ministry was drawing to an end, and there rested upon Him the responsibility of an awful decision. He had halted where the roads forked—which way should He take?

In a sermon preached a half dozen years ago I attempted to describe the two roads which Jesus faced that pivotal day, one of which He must take. I said in substance this: Two roads lay before our Lord; one was a ribbonlike highway that led to Nazareth, His old home town in the pleasant mountain region of Galilee; the other was a grim rocky road that led to Jerusalem where His enemies awaited His coming with well-wrought-out plans to destroy not only His influence but His life. One road led to Nazareth and peace, the other to Jerusalem and war. When He turned toward the road which led into Galilee, it was as if He heard soft music sweetly falling on the ear, and when He turned to the road that led to Jerusalem, it was as if He heard the solemn strains of a threnody, a dirge.

When I made that statement I believed it to be true; now I am sure I was wrong. I had some authority for that viewpoint, though I stated it in my own words. That is the view of at least one distinguished Scottish preacher whose books are eagerly read. Let me restate it: On the one hand, the road to peace and possibly a long life; on the other, the road to conflict and to die in manhood's morning. No, no, the decision was not as simple as that. How could it be? Few decisions of life really important are so simple; instead they are complex, intricate, baffling. Life is like that, as we soon discover.

Let this incident be faced squarely as we see it in perspective and as our own crucial experiences have unfolded to us the costliness of duty. Suppose Jesus had taken the road back to Galilee and by-passed the trials which awaited Him in Jerusalem. Could He have found peace in Nazareth, peace of mind, serenity of conscience? The answer is "No." How can anyone find peace who has taken the easier way out of a dilemma? Imagine Jesus returning to Nazareth knowing that He had chosen the wrong road, had purchased apparent peace, and saved His life at the price of cowardice. How could the process be otherwise than painful? Nor is it likely that His old home town would have received Him gladly. Following His temptation in the wilderness Jesus then returned to Nazareth. Though at first they received Him with admiration and pleasure, later some things that He said aroused their wrath, and they rose up and thrust Him out of the city. Might they not do so again? It is not always easy to go back home again to take up where one left off. Second pastorates are seldom successful. There's something in the proverbial expression "You can't go back home again."

Is it not plain the roads which Jesus faced cannot be so sharply contrasted as, say, the whiteness of the road to Nazareth, and the blackness of the road to Jerusalem? Each of these roads presented problems, offered difficulties, but with this vital moral difference: To travel the road back to Nazareth was wrong; to take the road to Jerusalem was right.

Jesus made the choice. He took not the low road to Nazareth, but the high road to Jerusalem. He had counted the cost. It was great, but not too great.

II

Jesus was advised not to go to Jerusalem. Simon Peter so admonished Him when in Caesarea Philippi Jesus announced that He must go to Jerusalem and suffer many things of the elders, chief priests, and scribes, be put to death, and rise again the third day. Jesus rebuked Simon sharply, saying, "Get thee behind me, Satan: thou art a stumbling-block unto me: for thou mindest not the things of God, but the things of men" (asv). G. Campbell Morgan had a vivid sermon on "The Falling Away of Simon

Peter from Christ." In that gifted preacher's mind this was the
beginning of his fall, for as Dr. Morgan put it: "He refused to
follow where he could not understand." It is probable that all of
the disciples of Jesus, Judas and Simon the Zealot excepted, because of their nationalistic ardor, advised their Master against
going up to Jerusalem, where the forces of opposition were en-
trenched and planning His destruction.

When we face our Jerusalem there will be many to advise us
one way or another, but at the long last, in lonely contemplation,
one must make his own decision for or against, to do or not to
do, to stay or to go, to hug the shore or to put out into the deep;
and the finer the character of the person who must make the
choice, the lonelier his state of suspense and struggle. No, I am
not forgetting Divine companionship; the pure in heart are sure
of that. I am speaking of well-meaning human beings who
would advise us to take the road that offered less opposition and
conflict. Their counsel is not to be despised, but the final decision often has to be made in utter loneliness of soul.

These inner conflicts are intimately known and experienced
by those who have ideals to live up to and an enlightened conscience to heed. Paul Laurence Dunbar in his "Ere Sleep Come
Down to Soothe the Weary Eyes" takes account of this struggle:

> Ere sleep come down to soothe the weary eyes,
> How questioneth the soul the other soul,—
> The inner sense which neither cheats nor lies,
> But self exposes unto self, a scroll
> Full writ with all life's acts unwise or wise,
> In characters indelible and known;
> So, trembling with the shock of sad surprise,
> The soul doth view its awful self alone,
> Ere sleep come down to soothe the weary eyes.

III

Let no one believe for a single careless moment that these
decisions Jesus made, which are part of the history of His public

ministry, were easily reached or that they did not cost Him struggle and tense inner conflict. The facts oppose this view. It has been held by some teachers of religion, though never accepted widely, and certainly not by the safest interpreters of the New Testament, that these experiences of Jesus, His acts, decisions, were as examples for us; that He was not really tempted, that He did not pray because He needed to pray; that He dramatized His mission in order to set a good example for those who would follow Him. It is surprising that such a view should win even a small following, for it takes the virility out of His nature, makes Him a play actor, devitalizes His life, and veneers it with artificiality.

Recall the incident in the Gospel narrative of His rising early in the morning and retiring into the mountains for prayer and communion. Behold Him saddened by the wrongs done to the poor and the humble by the powers of Church and State. See Him weeping at the grave of Lazarus. Hear Him exclaim in a voice choked with emotion, "O Jerusalem, Jerusalem, that killeth the prophets, and stoneth them that are sent unto her! how often would I have gathered thy children together, even as a hen gathereth her chickens under her wings, and ye would not!" (ASV).

Turn to the account of Jesus in the garden of Gethsemane and the soul struggle that took place there. Luke, who was a physician, describes His agony as He prayed beneath the olive trees through the branches of which the moonlight filtered. Here are the words the beloved physician wrote of that event, a description which he must have received from an eye witness: "And being in an agony he prayed more earnestly: and his sweat was as it were great drops of blood falling down to the ground." See, too, Hebrews 5:7: "Who in the days of his flesh, having offered up prayers and supplications with strong crying and tears unto him that was able to save him from death" (ASV).

Here is stark reality, no play acting; no pantomimic performance this, but awful agony, anguish, pain and suffering. The more sensitive a human being is, the more he suffers when a hurt is done him. A sharp, cruel word may be as a verbal sword thrust into the depths of his emotional nature and then twisted about so that it produces exquisite torture. Contemplate the sensitivity of the stainless character of Jesus and then estimate if you can the costliness of the struggles through which He went and the rough handling He received by word and deed of His enemies.

There are times when our Jerusalems exact much from us, handle us roughly, push us about ruthlessly, deflate our pride, and humble us to the earth. A disciple is not greater than his Master. If we live deeply, we cannot escape disappointment, disillusionment; but nothing that can happen to us can approach in awful poignancy what Jesus endured even before He came to His cross. One writer says that Jesus died to Himself in Gethsemane. If that is true, then the crucifixion touched only His physical being. The spirit had already its victory.

> There is a green hill far away,
> Without a city wall,
> Where the dear Lord was crucified,
> Who died to save us all.
>
> We may not know, we cannot tell
> What pains He had to bear,
> But we believe it was for us
> He hung and suffered there.

IV

One of the finest tributes ever paid Jesus fell from the lips of His enemies who milled about the foot of His cross. According to Mark, they were the church leaders of his day, the chief priests and the scribes. They mocked Him and said, "He saved others; himself he cannot save." Here is the law of the cross. Here is the New Commandment in action. Like a scarlet strand, this principle of losing one's life by saving others runs through the tapestry of history. If we think of this principle as a motif in a symphony, it appears both in major and minor strains. Faithful, devoted parents can save their children, but cannot save themselves. In times of depression, businessmen may save their businesses, but cannot save themselves. Men and women everywhere who possess ideals and follow the gleam are able to save some righteous cause, yet cannot save themselves. Unnumbered hosts have worn themselves out and died prematurely for others' sake, illustrating the law laid down by Jesus when He said, "Whosoever would save his life shall lose it; but whosoever shall lose his life for my sake, the same shall save it" (ASV).

"He saved others; himself he could not save." The truly noble in all generations knew the meaning of this rule of selfless living. In Athens, Greece, in the fabulous Age of Pericles, Socrates, born four hundred years before Christ, embodied in his life the truth of this tribute. Socrates was the grandest citizen of Athens, in spirit and in deed. Someone has said that in the purity of his teachings and conduct he reached out an arm's length toward Christ. But because he disbelieved in the pagan gods of Greece, he was voted by a small majority to die. He who had so often held out the cup of wisdom to all who would receive it was himself condemned to drink the cup of poisonous hemlock. He saved others, himself he could not save.

In John Drinkwater's *Abraham Lincoln* there is a dramatic scene, with Lincoln alone in his office in the White House. The Union had divided and the awful war was ravaging the nation. The President stands, gazing at a map hanging on the wall: a map of the United States of America. As he gazes upon it, he lifts his arms as if to take to his heart all of the states, North, South, East and West, in affectionate embrace. The gesture was symbolic. The Union he could save, himself he could not save.

In the city of Washington, in the early 1920's, in a house on S Street, a famed American sat in a wheel chair on the upstairs verandah at the rear of the house, overlooking at springtime the surroundings with cherry blossoms abloom over the city. He was a broken man, physically. One side of his face and body was paralyzed. There were lines of suffering in his long, lean face. His great day was over, and a little later men and women would kneel in front of his home where he lay dying. Woodrow Wilson could save the concept of a League of Nations to posterity, himself he could not save. One of President Wilson's favorite poems was the sad yet wholesome anonymous verses, *Dominus Illuminatio Mea,** two stanzas of which seem pertinent here:

> In the hour of death, after this life's whim,
> When the heart beats low, and the eyes grow dim,
> And pain has exhausted every limb—
> The lover of the Lord shall trust in Him.
>
> . . . .
>
> For even the purest delight may pall,
> And power must fail and pride must fall,
> And the love of the dearest friends grow small—
> But the glory of the Lord is all in all.

Our Lord saved others, Himself He could not save and save us, too.

V

No one is exempt from life's Jerusalems, not even those who stand in pre-eminent pulpits or serve at high altars. I recall some of the famed preachers of Christendom and pause to contemplate the Jerusalems to which they set out.

There was Chrysostom, "the golden-mouthed," possibly the greatest of early Christian preachers, who swept with his eloquence the multitudes that crowded the great church to hear him, first at Antioch and then at Constantinople. Yet, in the end the court at Constantinople turned savagely against him, and a wicked Empress banished him to faraway Armenia. At last, worn and weary, he begged that he be taken to a little

* Recently attributed to R. D. Blackmore.

wayside church that he might die, and his last words as he lay on the cold stone floor were "Glory to God in all things."

I think of Phillips Brooks and his truly marvelous preaching genius, honored and loved by millions; and I recall what Gaius Glenn Atkins wrote of this prophet of the Most High:

In the portraits of his early middle life he is a figure of radiant happiness, but his later portraits, beginning at fifty, show deepening lines. Thereafter the documentation of time is arresting; by fifty-five the eyes are sad and the lines are deep. A year later he is an old man. I know nothing like this in any other series of portraits, as though beneath all his fullness of apparently untroubled success, the price and passion of the Cross had had its way with him.

Now, Phillips Brooks has a sermon on "Going Up to Jerusalem," and I notice that Bishop William Scarlett includes it in his *Selected Sermons of Phillips Brooks*. A wise choice, for it is in this sermon, near the end, that there occurs one of the most precious and widely quoted sayings of that noble Servant of God. Seldom has so much been said in so few words:

O, do not pray for Easy lives. Pray to be stronger men! Do not pray for tasks equal to your powers. Pray for powers equal to your tasks! Then the doing of your work shall not be a miracle. But you shall be a miracle. Every day you shall wonder at yourself, at the richness of life which has come in you by the grace of God.

Here endeth the lesson.

9

The Most Unforgettable
Person I Know*

(A Preacher's Report to His Fellow Preachers)

He built no temple, yet the farthest sea
Can yield no shore that's barren of His place
  For bended knee.

He wrote no book, and yet His words and prayer
Are intimate on many myriad tongues,
  Are counsel everywhere.

The life He lived has never been assailed,
Nor any precept, as He lived it, yet
  Has ever failed.

He built no kingdom, yet a King from youth
He reigned, is reigning yet; they call His realm
  The kingdom of the Truth.

THERESE LINDSEY

IT IS with unaffected hesitancy that I speak on this subject so dear to my heart. Even though I bring my best to this theme, I realize I cannot do it full justice. There will be heights I cannot attain, and depths I cannot fathom. In such a spirit do I come to a discussion of "The Most Unforgettable Person I Know."

I

I was little more than a child when I first heard the name of this person, always spoken with reverence and something akin

---

* Delivered at Lynchburg College, Lynchburg, Virginia, March 9, 1948, in the Jennie Cutler Shumate Lectureship on the Christian Ministry.

to awe. I dimly recall being taken to a building that bore the name of this person and observing a man stand up and talk to the people about him. In our home were two or three copies of a highly prized book from which I heard stories read about this greatly revered man. By and by there was presented to me an illustrated copy of the much venerated book, and I saw for the first time an artist's conception of this unforgettable person. The first picture showed him surrounded by children on a hillside where flowers were plentiful. He was dressed in flowing robes and his hair fell in ringlets over his shoulders. The children about him were playful, perfectly at ease, laughing and talking and looking up into his face. The second picture showed him standing by the seashore and speaking to a throng of people who were listening with rapt attention. Back of him was a stretch of water on which was a sailboat and far away a distant shoreline, while overhead clouds, like ghost ships, were drifting by. These pictures held me as by a spell!

The years passed, and there came a Sunday when I sat in another building that had to do with this unforgettable person. A large, fine-looking man spoke impressively of his character, how he lived and loved and served. The speaker concluded with a warm, stirring appeal for those who had not yet publicly accepted this person's way of life, to do so that day. Something stirred within me to accept that invitation, and I moved out of the seat, up the aisle, and the fine-looking man took my small hand in his large hand. A little later he asked me if I was willing to take this noble character as the ideal of my young life and to make his standards of living my own. I answered in the affirmative, and that was a rememberable day for home folks, friends, neighbors, and for me!

The years swept by and I found myself, by influence both direct and subtle, deciding to commit my life to this unforgettable character and that for which he stood. There followed the preparation in a college where my teachers were men with the

graces, ideals and spirit of this world leader. The highly-prized
book in the home of my youth became the principal textbook,
and I listened to men of simple piety and sound learning, some
of whom came from afar to speak of this character and to inter-
pret him in classroom and chapel. One night I listened to a man
of patriarchal appearance who had gone with the story of this
character to the New Hebrides Islands—none other than John
G. Paton! He told us that when he first visited the islands the
inhabitants were cannibals, and at the end of his work there,
which was thirty years or more, the people had left off their
cannibalism and were devoted to the way of life this ineffable
person taught. It was an evening long to be cherished, and I
lived it over again and again. Those were golden months and
years, and when they were over, my comradeship with this person began in a still more intimate way, nor has it yet ended.

II

There came a time when I visited the country of this unforgettable person's birth. When our ship put in at a port city of
that land, a woman, as she stepped ashore, in a hysteria of joy,
fell prostrate and pressed her lips to the ground, fancying perhaps that the feet of this one she so adored once touched that
spot. She was a pilgrim who had come a long distance to visit
the memorable scenes and shrines of a country forever famed
in song and story, and her elation was understandable. I made
my way to the traditional place of this man's nativity. I passed
into a spacious and splendid church between rows of marble
columns, on up the central aisle to the emblazoned altar, and
turning to the right went down many steps to a cave where
fifty-three silver lamps were burning and numerous candles cast
fantastic shadows on the ancient walls. The stone walls were
blackened, and the tapestries which hung there were old and
encrusted with soot. There in the stone floor were the words in
Latin that said here was born this unforgettable character.

There in that historic place imagination carried me on swift pinions through many centuries to his natal day. Gone was the splendid church, and in its place an inn built over this cave, where livestock, cattle and horses and donkeys, were sheltered. That night of nights a peasant and his wife approaching her great hour, finding no room in the inn, were shown to this cave. And in that lowly place this person first saw the light of day, so tradition says.

As I left the church I gazed out over the near-by hills where David tended his father's flocks, and there came to my mind a certain famous hymn written by a fellow American, inspired by what he saw and the emotions he felt when he visited this shrine:

> O little town of Bethlehem,
> How still we see thee lie!
> Above thy deep and dreamless sleep
> The silent stars go by;
> Yet in thy dark streets shineth
> The everlasting Light;
> The hopes and fears of all the years
> Are met in thee tonight.

I journeyed to the town where this person was brought up, an attractive place in the hill country in the North. Here his boyhood was spent. Here he grew to man's estate. Close by this town is a high hill on which this dark-eyed youth must often have sat or stood. Before him unrolled like a huge tapestry the history of his nation. To the southwest the plains of Esdraelon and to the west the blue Mediterranean. To the north the Cedars of Lebanon and snow-capped Mount Hermon; to the east the Jordan Valley and the river hurrying on its way to meet the brackish waters of the Dead Sea; and in the distance the mountains that stand like sentinels guarding a land, small as mountains go, but great in history as shrines and memorials of events forever famed.

One afternoon I strolled to the place where a spring bubbles up and provides the water supply of the villagers—the same spring that bubbled up to quench the thirst of the townspeople when this youth lived there. It is a place, now as then, where the people gather to greet one another and perchance to pass along the latest gossip of the town. And I saw that day at this community center a comely matron with her water jar, and tugging at her skirts a dear, dark-eyed little boy, and I mused: "So it was with him and his mother at this spring, the long, long years ago."

The second night I spent in his old home town I separated myself from companions and went out upon the flat roof of the building where we were lodged. It was a moonlight night and the stars shone like great lanterns hung in the sky. Again I mused: "How often this person as boy and young man sat on some such roof and gazed upon these same stars, as he listened to the story of his nation, its poets, prophets, and lawgivers, as told by his elders."

Later I stood in the tawdry, ornate pile of masonry which is reported to be the place where this person died, and I thought how far removed this spectacle was in spirit from his life, teachings and ministry. From this stifling place it was a relief to seek out the section which lies beyond the walls where there is a hill and a tomb which bears a resemblance to that tomb in a garden where once his scarred body had rested. It was a Sunday morning, and a train of camels was passing along the road, their bells sweetly tinkling. . . . Now and then a donkey brayed, a rooster crowed; all else was quiet and serene. Sitting near this tomb with a group of friends we remarked on the quietness and the holy calm. It was as if we were at church and it was an Easter Lord's Day morning and the choir sang jubilantly of the victory over the grave!

III

Time glided by and I found myself in a quaint town in the Tyrolean Alps, where every ten years the pageant of this man's life is presented from a colossal stage. At eight o'clock on an August morning, I sat with five thousand visitors from the four points of the compass to see the Mighty Drama come to life. Before the huge curtain lifted, a chorus of three hundred men and women sang with fine effect, the men bearded, the women with hair unbound and falling over their shoulders. Then the pageantry began. Lo! the City of the Great King welcomed this person as he appeared in lowly estate, surrounded by little children singing hosannas, and his joyous friends rallying about him. I saw him enter the Temple, which had become a place of merchandising, and lo! he overturned the tables of the money-changers, released the doves from their prisons, and drove the livestock from the holy precincts, exclaiming as he did so: "My house shall be called the house of prayer; but ye have made it a den of thieves."

Thus I sat, with an hour's intermission at noon, the long day through as scene after scene passed: vivid, impressive, stirring. Then came the climactic scene in which was depicted with painful realism the last hours of this person's life; the last words he spoke; and then the great cry and—the awful end! The thousands of spectators sat in eloquent silence save for now and then a sob and a long-drawn sigh. Next, a Roman soldier thrust a spear into the left side of the still figure on the timbers and what appeared to be blood spattered upon the stage. At this a woman sitting near by softly, yet audibly, exclaimed: "O God! why did they let him die?"

Yet, after I left the tense packed building and came out into the open with the blue sky overhead, the mountain near by bearing on its summit a cross, and the westering sun flooding the village with golden rays, my thoughts turned to the simple villagers who played so well and so reverently the difficult parts. And I thought of the House of the Baker where we were guests and the gentle and kindly persons who saw to our needs in their modest home. For I saw and felt more of this unforgettable person's mind and spirit in these, our hosts, than I saw on the huge stage as the momentous scenes were enacted.

IV

It is time now to gather up some of the fundamental teachings that fell from the lips of this unforgettable person—teachings that were embodied in his way of life day after day.

How unforgettably this person spoke of God. No one before him or since has spoken so intimately of the Eternal. This is important, for we begin nowhere and we end nowhere unless God is in our thinking. Primitive man thought of God as a great Savage in the sky, capricious, vengeful, nor has that idea of God disappeared from the thinking of some in our own day. "For in fact old religions never die, they are merely driven under the surface." So spoke a noble interpreter of this person's life. "What is God like?" poses life's most basic question. Yet who of us can answer this question with finality? "A God defined is a God finished." This person had the answer. He spoke of himself as the portrait of the invisible God. "He that hath seen me hath seen the Father."

"God alone is permanently interesting," says Joseph Fort Newton, and there is the wisdom of truth in this quotable statement. Much that is around and about us is temporarily interesting but has its day and fades away. "How idle a boast after all, is the immortality of a name. . . . The idol of today pushes the hero of yesterday out of recollection; and will in turn, be supplanted by his successor of tomorrow." But Washington Irving was not thinking of this person or his name when he wrote so truthfully of the fickleness of human glory and fame.

There came a day when one of his closest friends asked this person for the explanation of a perplexing incident, and his reply was "Have faith in God." How unforgettably this person spoke of God when he said to those who came to listen to what he had to say on the deep things of life: "Be not anxious for your life, what ye shall eat, or what ye shall drink; nor yet for your body, what ye shall put on. Is not the life more than the food, and the body more than the raiment? . . . But if God doth so clothe the grass of the field, which to-day is, and to-morrow is cast into the oven, shall he not much more clothe you, O ye of little faith? . . . But seek ye first his kingdom and his righteousness; and all these things shall be added unto you" (ASV).

This person taught that our despair is God's opportunity. He did not say that God can make persons good without pain and struggle. He taught that God made us free to act, and that if we do wrong we must suffer for that wrong. He spoke of God as righteous, holy, just and merciful and taught that God's forgiveness is won through His children's penitence and obedience to His laws. And the wondrous truth about this person is that what he taught he was. Who other than this person could say, "God is like me," and strike no false note? Who else could say, "The Father and I are one," without an appalling incongruity? One other thing: It is unlikely that anyone who has written about God since this person lived has failed to consider his teaching about God, so indelibly has this person impressed the theologians.

How unforgettably this person spoke of man. He knew what was in man. He knew the heights to which man can soar; the nobleness that within him lies; the hero that is in the soul of man. And he knew also the depths of degradation to which man can fall, the red-hot passions that can master him. And yet withal he spoke of man as made in God's image, as part of an eternal plan. Then there is the story he told of a shepherd who had a hundred sheep, and when he gathered them within the fold at nighttime one sheep was missing. Did the shepherd say, "Well, ninety-nine sheep are here, what matter if one is missing"? Not so. He could not rest until he and his helpers had gone out into the night and searched until they found the missing sheep and brought him safely home to the fold.

When this person had finished this story he made this comment: "How much better than a sheep is a man." The implications of this statement are staggering. When this person came to earth not many human beings counted; only the powerful, the learned and the rich counted; the masses of the people counted not at all, but in the minds of those who rated highly, were as so many "dumb driven cattle." This person taught that every man, woman and child counted. And that, too, was, and still is, revolutionary doctrine.

As for the children, he loved them and they loved him dearly. Two scenes in his life deserve to be put on many a canvas, as indeed they have been and will continue to be the subject of painters and poets too. Once when his closest friends were quarreling as to which should be the greatest in the kingdom which they expected him to set up, this lover of little children called to a child loitering near by, and setting him in their midst, said, "Verily I say unto you, Except ye turn, and become as little children, ye shall in no wise enter into the kingdom of heaven. Whosoever therefore shall humble himself as this little child, the same is the greatest in the kingdom of heaven. And whoso shall receive one such little child in my name receiveth me: but whoso shall cause one of these little ones that believe on me to stumble, it is profitable for him that a great millstone should be hanged about his neck, and that he should be sunk in the depth of the sea" (ASV). Then, too, recall that day when the women were bringing him their little boys and girls that he might put his hands on their heads and bless them. His friends belittled the request of the mothers and were sending the children away, but when this person saw it he was moved and indignant, and said, "Suffer the little children to come unto me; forbid them not: for to such belongeth the kingdom of God. . . . And he took them in his arms, and blessed them" (ASV).

V

How vividly I recall the day I first came across George Mac-Donald's precious poem based on this incident of Jesus blessing little children. I was in my first city pastorate, at Cleveland,

Ohio, and very young. The poem fascinated me. I memorized it and wished to quote it, but the broad Scottish dialect in which it was written troubled me, for I am an Irish Welshman, with only a wee drop of the Scottish in me. Then I had an inspiration. I hunted up a Scottish Presbyterian preacher I knew, put the poem in his hands and said: "Would you be so kind as to read this poem for me?" He did so. "Please read it again," I urged; and when I asked him to listen to me read, and be free to criticize, he made but a few suggestions, and I have been quoting MacDonald's lovely lines ever since:

> The Maister sat in a wee cot house
> Tae the Jordan's watters near,
> An' the fisherfolk crush'd an' croodet roon
> The Maister's words tae hear.
>
> An' even the bairns frae near-han streets
> Kept mixin' in wi' the thrang,
> Laddies and lassies wi' wee bare feet,
> Jinkin' the crood amang.
>
> An' ane o' the twal' at the Maister's side
> Ris up an' cried alood:
> "Come, come, bairns, this is nae place for you,
> Rin awa' hame oot o' the crood."
>
> But the Maister said, as they turned tae go,
> "Lat the wee bairns coom tae Me."
> An' He gaithert them roon Him whaur He sat,
> An' lifted ane up on His knee.
>
> Aye, He gaithert them roon Him whaur He sat,
> An' He straikit their curly hair,
> An' He said to the wunnerin' fisherfolk
> Wha croodet aroon Him there:
>
> "Send na the weans awa' frae Me,
> But raither this lesson learn,
> That nane'll win in at heaven's yett*
> Wha is na as puir's a bairn."

* Gate.

An' He that has taen us for kith and kin,
Tho' a Prince o' the far awa',
Gaithert them roon Him whaur He sat,
An' blisset them ane an' a'.

The attitude of this remarkable person toward women in general and their wayward sisters in particular was such as to set him apart from his contemporaries. He treated courtesans with the same respect he gave to the women of social and synagogal standing. Others might scorn and ostracize those of easy virtue, but to such this person said: "Go thy way, from henceforth sin no more." While in his radiant presence these wayward ones were again gentlewomen.

One day as this person sat by a well, famous in his country's history, a woman from a neighboring town came with her water jar to refill it. Since she bore a tarnished reputation, his friends were dismayed when he engaged her in friendly conversation. Beginning with the errand which had brought her to the well, he lifted the theme to spiritual heights and spoke of the water of life, which if one drinks he will nevermore thirst, nor did he conceal from her his knowledge of the kind of life she was living. When the conversation ended, the woman left her water jar and ran to tell her fellow villagers the wonderful thing which had happened to her, saying, "Could this be the one we are looking for?" Thus it came about that this woman with a past became a woman with a future after she had talked with a person she could never forget.

VI

How unforgettably this person spoke of Life Eternal, here and hereafter. He did not speak of a city where there were "golden streets," "gates of pearl," and "jasper walls." These are flashes of splendid imagery, but they were not in this person's vocabulary. Instead, he spoke of his "Father's house," a homey term which everybody can understand and appreciate. In the

Father's house, he said, there are many "mansions" or "apartments," a spacious, roomy place. This earth must be one of these mansions, and how many other apartments there are in the Father's house no one can say or imagine. Once he said to a companion in suffering, replying to his plaintive request, "Remember me when thou comest into thy kingdom," "Today thou shalt be with me in paradise." No one knows where paradise is, but the promise of being with this unforgettable one is ineffably comforting. Again, this person once said, "I am the door." Ponder this figure, for it merits contemplation. A door is an introduction to what it opens into, and as is the door so is the building. If the door is battered, hanging on a single hinge, then he who would enter knows he is about to pass into a dilapidated building. On the other hand, if the door is polished and beautiful, he knows it opens into an edifice also beautiful and attractively furnished. If this person is the door to eternal life here and hereafter, what more could one ask or desire?

Nancy Byrd Turner may have had this phrase "I am the door" in mind when she wrote her lovely lines entitled "Death Is a Door":

> Death is only an old door
> Set in a garden wall.
> On quiet hinges it gives at dusk,
> When the thrushes call.
>
> Along the lintel are green leaves;
> Beyond, the light lies still;
> Very weary and willing feet
> Go over that sill.
>
> There's nothing to trouble any heart,
> Nothing to hurt at all.
> Death is only an old door
> In a garden wall.

That poem could never have been written had not this unforgettable person come into this world and by his teaching and way of life flooded with a mellow light the question, "If a man die shall he live again?"

Louise Chandler Moulton must have had this unforgettable person in mind when she wrote:

> Some day or other I shall surely come
> Where true hearts wait for me;
> Then let me learn the language of that home
> While here on earth I be,
> Lest my poor lips for want of words be dumb
> In that High company.

The good news is that we can "learn the language of that home." What better teacher can we find than this unforgettable teacher? For we come to know him by faith and through experience. The story of his life is not only in *the* book but also in myriad other books. It is graven in stone, portrayed on canvas, diffused through many channels and, best of all, etched in the noble characters of an unnumbered host. Of the making of many books about this person there is no end, and much study about him is refreshing to body and soul. And in such High Company we cannot but speak the things which we have heard and seen and felt.

VII

How unforgettably this person died and how impossible it was for death to destroy him. Who can be glib or casual when he surveys this last scene and attempts to tell what happened there? "If you have tears prepare to shed them now" and for greater cause than those who wept by Caesar's coffin. "Greater love hath no man than this, that a man lay down his life for his friends." For love can do no more than die, save to die in the cruelest and saddest way. "He saved others, himself he could not save." How little he who uttered this bitter taunt could realize the ineffable tribute he paid the one who suffered there.

10

The Mantle of Charity

And Noah began to be an husbandman, and he planted a vine-yard: and he drank of the wine, and was drunken; and he was uncovered within his tent. And Ham, the father of Canaan, saw the nakedness of his father, and told his two brethren without. And Shem and Japheth took a garment, and laid it upon both their shoulders, and went backward, and covered the nakedness of their father; and their faces were backward, and they saw not their father's nakedness.   GENESIS 9:20-23

I DO not recall having heard or read a sermon based on this Old Testament incident. I readily agree with the fastidious that this is not a decorous scene to look upon. Drunkenness never is pleasant to behold. A drunken man deep in his cups is often an object such as to move angels to tears, if angels ever weep. There is a story of a proud man who once boasted that he had never committed certain major sins, three in number. Then he got drunk, and his mind maddened by alcohol, he committed all three. Shakespeare, in his tragedy of Othello, makes Cassio say: "O God, that men should put an enemy in their mouths to steal away their brains."

The one factor in this sorry scene which lifts it out of grossness and invests it with decency is the deed of Noah's sons in taking a garment and walking backward with averted eyes and covering the naked body of their father as he lay sprawled out in a drunken stupor.

On the whole, the Mantle of Charity is not often in evidence in the Old Testament. That literature is starkly realistic. If we had been writing about Abraham, Jacob and David, we would have glossed over certain wrongdoings of which they were guilty, or omitted them altogether. But the chroniclers of the

129

Old Testament told the truth about their heroes, shocking though it sometimes was.

In this frank portrayal of human frailties the New Testament differs from the Old. Not that the New glosses over wrongdoing; not at all. The deadly wages of sin are set down, and the dire consequences of evil traced "in characters indelible and known." Still, as a rule, the climate of the New Testament is gentler and more favorable to justice tempered with mercy than the Old. But of this more later on.   *transition*

I

Like the quality of Mercy, the ministry of the Mantle of Charity is twice blest. It blesses him who gives and him who takes. In truth, the mantling of charity about the human frailties of others is itself a mark of mercy—is love in action. Old Diogenes is pictured going about with a lantern looking for an honest man. He could have found that kind of a man without a lantern had he looked in the right places. But Diogenes, with his lantern, could not have found a faultless person; no more can we, although we may turn a powerful, dazzling searchlight on humanity.

Imagine what would happen if human beings spoke in public their opinions and criticisms of one another which they speak guardedly in private, or the uncharitable thoughts they cherish but do not put in words. Imagine the consequences! Families would disintegrate, churches become discordant and in turmoil, communities belligerent and embroiled in strife. Why, life would be unendurable. It is the understanding heart, the tempered spirit, the guarded tongue, the love that "thinketh no evil," which holds the family together, unifies the Church, and saves the community and the state from dissolution.

Take a close-up view of our heroes, not for the purpose of "debunking"—how I dislike this word, but it is in the dictionaries and its meaning familiar to us all. Some of our heroes had feet of clay, and all of them being human had faults and weaknesses. So far as our truly great are involved, their frailties were as spots on a glorious sun. It may be that this fact brings them closer to us and we love them all the more.

Look at Martin Luther. There he stands in history: a titanic figure. We owe him much. He set on foot human liberations that shook the world. Our democracy as well as our Protestantism is in unpayable debt to this sturdy German, who faced alone the powers of Church and State. Yet he had his faults. He sometimes threw wild words around carelessly. He was obstinate and not always easy to work with. The one big splotch on his escutcheon is his failure to side with the poor and the disinherited in the Peasants' War, choosing rather to stand with the powerful, the nobles, and on the side of the highly placed. Yet, we throw the Mantle of Charity over Luther's mistakes. His virtues and his accomplishments far outnumber and outweigh his weaknesses. We have to take our public men as we find them, and if they are honest and faithful to the larger tasks, we forget and forgive their minor faults.

And there is Lincoln! Now and then somebody wonders if we have not deified him. No, that was not possible. He was too human, too much of the earth, earthy. He was not a demigod. He had his weaknesses, frailties. They were known to his friends. They were better known to himself. But what trivial foibles they were, what peccadilloes. And who cares to recall them save to show the great human being Lincoln was.

And what of Franklin D. Roosevelt? It may require two generations before his ministrations to a broken world and measures to better the conditions of the underprivileged can be justly weighed and fairly appraised. Not until those who idolized him and those who hated him have passed from off the earthly scene can justice be done the man and his works. Time may have its way with him as it has had with Jefferson, Jackson, Cleveland and other embattled Presidents. For the present the Mantle of Charity should be ample enough to cover the ambivalence of F.D.R. and likewise the animosity of his detractors.

There was once a famous American statesman whose political life was embattled, and he missed the grand prize—the Presidency. In his latter years, in conversation with a young newspaperman who had come to interview him, he took the reporter to a window overlooking a wooded park. "See the trees," he said, "how beautiful they look from here, but if you examine them closely you will find ugly knots, broken branches and dead limbs. So it is with men in public life. Better look at them from a distance, and credit them for what good they have done, and forget their faults and frailties." There is something in this; the Mantle of Charity is in the word picture that statesman painted.

II

Not only is it necessary to walk backward and spread the Mantle of Charity over individuals, we are obliged to do likewise with movements, organizations, crafts and the world of business, professions and vocations in general. Unity of opinion and viewpoint do not anywhere exist in our democratic institutions; controversy and dissent are ever at work, without which progress would be impossible, although we deplore the methods and the manners which so often disturb and discourage us. The political world is nearly always in disruption, and Presidential campaigns, nightmares four months long. Yet, this is democracy at work. It is not working as smoothly and as righteously as we could wish, but it is working, and what is more, we work with it and vote as we choose. Over the excesses, puerilities, banalities and sometimes hypocrisies, we throw the Mantle of Charity, remembering that out of such strange and uncouth methods we have discovered and put in office a Jackson, a Lincoln and a Cleveland. Fisher Ames, one of the Founding Fathers of our Republic, was right: "A democracy is like a raft, hard to steer, and your feet are always wet."

Coming closer home, behold my own beloved brotherhood, the Disciples of Christ! Born of a prayer for the unity of the churches, we are split among ourselves three ways. It would be easy to throw up our hands in despair and cry, "a plague on all three houses." But we do well to remember that the note of unity which our pulpits sounded almost alone for a century has brought forth results. Now with few exceptions that note of unity is being sounded clear and strong by the major denominations. We have not lived in vain as a communion. Who knows but the striking of this note of reunion in season and out of season had much to do with Amsterdam and the World Council of Churches. We have much to praise in our movement for the unity of the divided House of God; and over the divisions and controversies among our brethren we throw the Mantle of Charity, saying humbly betimes, "To know all is to forgive all."

Forgiveness is the forgotten fundamental.

III

It is time we turn to the New Testament, where the climate is especially favorable to the Mantle of Charity and where it is so often in beneficent use. One is embarrassed by the wealth of teaching, incident and illustration on the side of compassion, forgiveness, mercy without stint, which he finds in this Christian literature. Only a few instances out of many are cited here, incidents so notable, so tender, so full of compassion as should move the dullest heart.

The enemies of Jesus brought a woman taken in adultery into His presence, saying, "Master, in the law Moses commanded us to stone such persons. What therefore dost thou say?" Now these accusers were not concerned about the morals of Jerusalem. They were eager to trap Jesus, confound Him, and lessen His influence. Did they expect Him to berate the woman and commend her accusers? If so, they were due to have the surprise of their lives. Jesus stooped and wrote in the sand. The episode was a brazen act on the part of her accusers. There was the woman, broken and harassed, at His feet. He stooped and silently wrote in the dust. They continued to ask Him, "What are you going to do with this woman?" He raised himself up

and said: "Let him that is without sin among you be the first
to cast a stone at her." And again He stooped down and wrote
on the ground. Hearing this unexpected reply, the accusers
went away, one by one, beginning with the oldest. Jesus and the
woman were left alone. He raised Himself up and said to her,
"Has no one condemned thee?" She answered: "No one, Lord."
Then said Jesus, "Neither do I condemn thee. Go thy way and
sin no more."* Was ever the Mantle of Charity more gently
draped over an erring human being?

> O Love divine, that stooped to share
> Our sharpest pang, our bitt'rest tear!

There is the case of Peter, who, in an hour of crisis both for
his Master and himself, denied that he was a follower of Jesus,
denied that he even so much as knew Him, and accompanied
the denials with rude oaths. On the seashore the Christ came to
Simon Peter and gave him the opportunity to confess Him
thrice, in the memorable words, "Thou knowest I love thee."
And on the day of Pentecost it was none other than Simon Peter
who was the spokesman, the preacher of the first Christian
sermon ever delivered. Nor is there likelihood that any of his
fellow Christians took him aside after that notable service he
rendered that day to say in envy or downright meanness, "See
here, Peter, don't you remember that you are the one who on a
certain fateful night denied your Lord three times? Why, you
even denied with an oath that you knew Him." No, so far as
we know, nothing happened like that to dim the splendor of
that day—the birthday of the Church. His fellow Christians
threw the Mantle of Charity about that shabby episode and
never referred to it again. Simon Peter, like many another erring disciple of our Lord, rose on "stepping stones of his dead
self to higher things."

* There was no need for Jesus to condemn her, for she had already
condemned herself. . . . Further condemnation would have been
unnecessary and cruel.—Leslie D. Weatherhead in *When the Lamp
Flickers.*

Then there was Judas, who betrayed His Lord. John, in after years, remembered that at the Last Supper, Jesus dipped the bread in the sop and gave it to him who had already bargained to sell his Master to the enemies. Now, for a host to dip the bread in the sop and hand it to a guest was to do that guest a signal honor, to choose him as the favored guest. By that gesture it was as though Jesus said to Judas, "You see I love you, Judas. Now can you do this thing to me? Judas, I love you." Was not this unprecedented courtesy a mantling of the would-be betrayer with a love that was reluctant to let him go on with the wicked bargain? For one, I think so. And at the bitter end, with the shouts of derision and jeers of those who willed that He should die upon the cross, Jesus prayed, "Father forgive them for they know not what they do." Was ever so ineffable a mantle of charity divine flung over the madding mob that clamored for his blood?

The Mantle of Charity! What a theme! Who can do justice to it? It occurs to me that I have said but a little of the much that could be said on so vast and neglected a subject. But I hope I have said enough perchance to soften the hard heart that is stubbornly set against justice, compassion, mercy and forgiveness.

> So let me draw you to the Great Forgiveness
> Not as one who stoops to save you,
> Not as one who stands aside with counsel;
> Nay, as one who says, "I too was poisoned
> With the flowers that sting, but now arisen,
> I am struggling up the path beside you;
> Rise and let us face these heights together."

11

The Greatening of
Abraham Lincoln*

Thy gentleness hath made me great.
2 SAMUEL 22:36
He endured, as seeing him who is invisible.
HEBREWS 11:27

IN THE backwoods of Kentucky, on the twelfth day of February, 1809, in a one-room cabin with a dirt floor and lighted by a single window, Abraham Lincoln was born. From that lowly birth he climbed through struggle and sorrow to the stars of fame and greatness, so that to the ends of the earth the inspiring story of his life has gone to thrill and ennoble millions. To unnumbered hosts, to think of America is to remember Lincoln, and to recall his name is to think of the land that gave him birth. It is profitable to consider the greatening of his character, both as a statesman and as a man among men.

The fifty-six years of Abraham Lincoln's life fall into four well-defined periods: seven years in Kentucky, fourteen years in Indiana, thirty-one in Illinois, and four at Washington as President. Here is the epic of America in four stages, scenes, acts. Kentucky: birth and childhood; Indiana: youth and young manhood; Illinois: maturity and national leadership; Washington: the purgatorial years of suffering, and the chief citizen receives the martyr's crown.

Lincoln's preparation for public life began early. The very

* Awarded first prize, 1939, in the Abraham Lincoln sermon contest, set up by the estate of the late Dr. John D. Long, distinguished clergyman, author and Lincoln scholar.

air that he breathed as a boy and young man was freighted with
political controversy and the issues that were destined to stir
the nation to its depths. Certain books were factors in his for-
tunes. Judge Wanamaker says that Lincoln learned the ethical
side of government from the Holy Scriptures. It may well be
true. He knew the Bible, and no man in American life has
quoted from it so freely and so effectively.

He was a mere boy when he began to study the Declaration
of Independence. He analyzed it. He took its doctrines apart
and scrutinized them. He quoted oftener from Thomas Jefferson
than from any other statesman. He loved to muse over those
thrilling words: "We hold these truths to be self-evident: that
all men are created equal, that they are endowed by their
Creator with certain unalienable Rights, that among these are
Life, Liberty and the pursuit of Happiness."

Lincoln studied the Constitution of the United States; he
pored long hours over the *Revised Statutes of Indiana*. These
are not textbooks, though he used them as such. He seems to
have loved their legal phrasings, the epigrammatic force of some
of the sentences. He saw in these documents something more
than printed pages. He beheld the country itself, a nation of
breathing souls, not having yet attained unto the ideals of the
Fathers. There was romance in these political papers. He read
them, not for the hour or the day, but for all time. Instead of
reading books interpreting these historic writings, he went to
the fountain itself.

In his Indiana days young Lincoln came into possession of
Weems' *Life of Washington*. He read it many times. It is likely
that he could recite whole sections of it from memory. Weems'
book is now derided by many who forget that there is gold along
with the dross in its chapters. Lincoln saw nothing absurd in
this book, nothing to laugh at, but much to praise and remember. It probably never occurred to him to question the cherry-
tree incident or to doubt that, in the awful winter at Valley

Forge, Washington unburdened himself before Almighty God in prayer. The Lincoln of this period was a hero worshiper and, I think, in a modified form, was so until the day of his death.

He was early getting into politics. He ran for the legislature in 1832, when he was but twenty-three years of age. He was defeated. He ran again in 1834, and was elected. He served four terms in all in the legislature of Illinois, was elected to Congress over Peter Cartwright in 1846, was a Presidential elector on the Whig ticket in 1844, and made speeches for Henry Clay. He campaigned for Scott in 1852, was defeated for the United States Senate in 1855, was a Presidential elector on the Republican ticket in 1856, and campaigned for John C. Fremont. He was nominated for the United States Senate by his party in 1858, and out of this came the debates with Douglas that made Lincoln a national figure. He was defeated, but in that defeat his victory for the Presidency was assured. Elected in 1860 as chief magistrate of the nation, he was re-elected in 1864. Thus the preparation for citizenship in Kentucky, expedited and enriched in Indiana, was followed by thirty-one years of politics, lawmaking, officeholding, and the practice of law.

The greatening of Lincoln's political philosophy is an arresting study. The student of his speeches and public papers is embarrassed by the wealth of material. I select one paragraph from a message to Congress, not so familiar to the rank and file as other Lincoln addresses, despite the fact that it was an important deliverance. This message was prepared by Mr. Lincoln at the outset of the Civil War, and this particular paragraph contains what I should call the quintessence of his political principles:

This is essentially a people's contest. . . . It is a struggle for maintaining in the world that form and substance of government whose leading object is to elevate the condition of men—to lift artificial weights from the shoulders, to clear the paths of laudable pursuits for all, to afford all an unfettered start and a fair chance in the race of life. Yielding to partisan and temporary departure from necessity, this after all is the leading object of the government for whose existence we contend.

Here are four mighty affirmations of a political creed truly Lincolnian. They are worthy much pondering since they are fundamental in the life of a republic. Take the first: "To elevate the condition of men." This is basic democracy. It is applied Christianity also. In the synagogue of his home town, Jesus selected a passage from the Prophet Isaiah and applied the same to himself. Who can forget those eloquent words?

The Spirit of the Lord is upon me, because he hath anointed me to preach the gospel to the poor; he hath sent me to heal the broken-hearted, to preach deliverance to the captives, and recovering of sight to the blind, to set at liberty them that are bruised.

Here Lincoln affirms that it is the object of such a government as ours to better conditions of living. Was he thinking of the several kinds of serfdom that endanger a people—industrial, social, economic? Was there especially in his mind the condition of four millions of Negroes, victims of slavery? The answer is "yes" to both questions.

Second: "To lift artificial weights from the shoulders." The word "artificial" is used here with discrimination. What about the "natural" rights of men? Lincoln is getting back to the Declaration of Independence. Consider the artificial burdens that rest heavily on drooping shoulders, unjust systems of taxation, iniquitous tariffs, unfair and discriminating legislation. Whatever weighs down the backs of men with burdens that are intolerable, it is the high business of a government by the people and for the people to remove. And it is something that is never finished; it must be a long-drawn-out process, "eternal vigilance," ceaseless endeavor, building like corals, grave on grave.

Third: "To clear the paths of laudable pursuits for all." It would seem a paradox that in a democracy the paths of laudable pursuits would ever be cluttered up by obstructions that would hinder the humblest citizen in the pursuit of happiness. But a democracy does not miraculously change human nature. Men are essentially the same under any form of government. Human passions and selfishness persist whatever the system of government. Of political blowers of bubbles, we have an embarrassing host. A democracy must be interested in clearing paths, blazing highways, cutting channels, that the spirit of the people, their hopes and dreams, may find free course and be fruitful.

Fourth: "To afford all an unfettered start and a fair chance in the race of life." This may seem a repetition of what has already been stated, but it is not. Rather, it is an amplification. The first few years of life practically settle destiny; and "an unfettered start" would mean wholesome food, adequate shelter and clothing. It would mean education. It would mean every man's opportunity. We have not yet achieved such a happy state of affairs. Great hosts of our citizens are fettered at the start, handicapped in the race of life by conditions which they did not make and over which they have no control. Mr. Lincoln knew from experience how hard it is to rise above the level of one's environment. He knew that slavery was wrong and averred that no man, however good, is good enough to own another human being. He believed that politicians should take their case to the people and he held with Jefferson that, if the people were informed, the people would not go far wrong.

In connection with a consideration of Mr. Lincoln's ideas of democracy, it is interesting to know that one who listened to his address at Gettysburg observed he did not in that mighty closing sentence put the emphasis where most of us do. Usually we emphasize it this way: "This nation, under God, shall have a new birth of freedom, and that government *of* the people, *by* the people, *for* the people, shall not perish from the earth." But a close observer who was present reports that Mr. Lincoln emphasized it thus: "that government of the *people*, by the *people*, for the *people*, shall not perish from the earth."

Abraham Lincoln's greatening ideals of governmental affairs included the belief that God is, and that he is a rewarder of them who seek him. Lincoln's religion has been the subject of innumerable controversies, some of them acrimonious and, withal, unwarranted. For, by his own writings and undisputed utterance, he wrote and talked as a man of faith and prayer. He may have been skeptical in the old Salem and early Springfield days. Who of us has not known seasons when religion seemed remote and trust in God not yet a fact of experience? Lincoln's faith grew; it grew slowly and flowered during those terrible years of the Presidency, until that faith became the strongest force in his life, as he bore the awful burden of state and struggled to preserve the integrity of the Federal Union.

Mr. Lincoln often referred to the precepts of Christianity; what is more important, he practiced them. We do not know what theories of prayer he held for he never explained; we only know that during his Presidency he was a praying man. Once he told a delegation of ministers that he conceived of prayer as bringing him to the side of God, not as winning God over to his side. He believed in One whom he sometimes called "That Divine Being," and again, "The Almighty Architect." The subtle creeds and fine-spun theological speculations so rife in his day troubled and perplexed him. He once said, in answer to a question as to why he was not a member of the church, "When any church will inscribe over its altar, as its sole qualification for membership, the Saviour's condensed statement of the substance of both law and gospel, 'Thou shalt love the Lord thy God with all thy heart, and with all thy soul, and with all thy mind, and thy neighbor as thyself,' that church will I join with all my heart and all my soul."

It may be said by way of comment on this quotation that the statement of Jesus with respect to the law and the gospel is written on the altars of all the churches, but so much else is also written there that is secondary and relatively unimportant that the fundamental teachings of Jesus are obscured. Slowly and surely this man's faith deepened, expanded, flowered.

When Lincoln lay dead and the country was racked with

grief and anxiety, James A. Garfield addressed from the balcony of a New York hotel a throng of excited and sorrow-stricken citizens. "God reigns," he said, "and the government at Washington still lives." It might profit us today to affirm that the government as conceived by our fathers lives only so long as it remembers that God reigns.

It is interesting to trace the greatening of Lincoln's literary style. It grew gradually and flowered in the period of the Presidency. His earlier speeches were forceful and often quaint but gave little promise of his masterpieces. He experimented with the ornate and with the long periodic sentence type of speech, found it not to his liking, and soon discarded it. He began to simplify his style, favored shorter sentences, exercised brevity, and the result was rewarding.

His letters throughout his life, on the whole, are models of brevity and condensation. The clarity of his speech, which from the beginning of his public life was observable, improved until in the end it was well-nigh perfect. Sometimes he was laconic.

Mr. Lincoln's style of speech in the famous debates with Senator Douglas is colloquial, informal, varied, and often marked by apt local allusions readily understood and appreciated by his hearers. But the clarity is there, the logic is in evidence, and all the time the speaker was growing, becoming more experienced, surer of himself. It is not possible to overpraise these debates and their greatening influence on Abraham Lincoln as a powerful public speaker.

The most famed of Mr. Lincoln's literary and oratorical compositions are, in the order named, the Farewell Address on leaving Springfield, the First Inaugural, the Gettysburg Address, the letter to Mrs. Bixby, and the Second Inaugural. In these the style is pellucid, simple, majestic, and at times distinguished by a sublime Biblical strain. But there are numerous other speeches and letters that deserve to be studied as specimens of his growing effectiveness in the use of the English language. There is the Cooper Union Address, his longest public speech, in which Lincoln won for himself a new following among the scholarly and cultured Eastern statesmen and other men of affairs. That speech, as delivered, began badly and ended grandly. The argument is strong, swift moving, conciliatory and logical. The orator rose to great heights of moral grandeur in the peroration and sat down victor in a difficult environment.

Where did Lincoln get his style? This is a question often asked. The answer is that he developed it through painstaking care and study of models of the best compositions. Unquestionably his familiarity with *Pilgrim's Progress, Robinson Crusoe* and the best poetry influenced his style—and, above all, his constant reading of the Bible, from which he quoted often and impressively. And the weight of the awful responsibilities he carried as the head of a divided and warring nation, together with his sensitivity toward suffering and sorrow, imparted something to his letters and speeches that not even those wells of English undefiled could bestow—a nobility of spirit, Christlike in gentleness and compassion.

The moral grandeur of Lincoln was both an endowment and an achievement. His lineage was better than some of his biographers would have us believe. Back of this son of the wilderness is a long line of sturdy, God-fearing ancestors. Note the Biblical names that appear in this family: Abraham, Enoch, Mordecai, Levi and the like. Thomas Lincoln came upon hard times because of the death of his father at the hands of marauding Indians and the fact that the huge tract of Kentucky land which he owned was lost through inability to clear the title. There was the stuff of virile manhood in young Abraham, and this he developed and refined in the school of hardship, privation, and disappointment. Nobody presented him anything on a silver platter, not even the Presidency.

It was in the early Salem days that he was first called "Honest Abe." Usually a boy who is honest in little things will grow into a man whose honesty is equal to the day of large things. Thus, to the larger issues of life, Mr. Lincoln brought the same punctilious concern as was in evidence in the old days at New Salem, when he trudged three miles to the home of a woman customer and back to restore the sum of six and one-quarter cents that was due her. His partner failing to meet the obligations of the business adventure in that village store, Lincoln assumed the full responsibility. It took him seventeen years to pay off this obligation, to which he humorously referred as "the national debt."

Mr. Lincoln cared little for money, defining wealth as a "superfluity of what we don't need." His fees were small, even where large ones were warranted. Nor could he bring himself to take a case where the ethics were suspect. When Mr. Lincoln ran for Congress in 1846, his friends presented him with an expense fund of $200. After the election, he returned $199.25 to the donors, explaining that he had spent seventy-five cents for cider, with which he treated a group of harvest hands at work in a field. Perhaps there is no lesson that this generation needs so much to take to heart as this one of common honesty, so bedrock in the life of the Civil War President.

Lincoln was patient with his plodding father, patient with his high-strung wife, patient with his lively children, patient with the scholarly and sometimes presumptuous Secretary Seward, with the fiery and irascible Secretary Stanton, with the imperious and ambitious Secretary Chase, patient with the haughty and arrogant General McClellan. He was patient with the preachers who urged him to take more decisive action, with the politicians who were always on his flank trying to goad him into momentous decisions before the time was ripe. He was patient with himself and, I say it reverently, patient with God.

In some respects the loveliest tribute ever paid this "homely hero" was that of Colonel Robert G. Ingersoll: "Lincoln was the grandest figure of the fiercest civil war. He is the gentlest memory of our world." The goodness of his heart was such as to bewilder his foes. In a letter to his friend Joshua Speed, he wrote: "I have never knowingly planted a thorn in any human heart, but I have always endeavored to pluck a thorn and plant a flower wherever a flower would grow." And from the soil of this man's personality, watered by tears and enriched by sorrow, sprang into life and flowered this sentiment: "With malice toward none, with charity for all, with firmness in the right, as God gives us to see the right, let us strive on to finish the work we are in." Verily, his gentleness has made us great.

Abraham Lincoln's soul greatened under the burdens he bore as President. Up to that time his religious life was not deep or serious, though his morals were excellent. His cardinal virtues were Christian all through the years. But it was not until he passed through these purgatorial years that the dross of his character fell away, and what remained seemed pure gold. He leaned hard upon the Everlasting Arms; he bowed humbly in the presence of the Eternal and prayed for light that he might walk in the path of truth and justice. He heard the news of the success of the Northern armies with gratitude but without exultation. Peace, peace, at last! How best to bind up the nation's wounds and to care for the widow and the orphan; how best to reunite in unseverable bonds the nation that had been broken—this he was brooding over when, lo! a shot rang out, and "prophecy was dumb!"

Abraham Lincoln was not a demigod. He was human. He had his weaknesses. His foibles were well known to his friends; they were better known to himself. Yet his imperfections were trivial compared with his basic virtues. His flaws were as spots on a glorious sun. They do not so much as touch the grand qualities that made him what he was. Consider the elements that so mixed in him as to give him an Olympian stature:

He was tolerant. He was temperate. He was generous. He was merciful. He was magnanimous. He was forgiving. He was just. He was gentle. He was kind. He was faithful. He was honest. He was humble. He was patient. He was diligent. He was truthful. He was prayerful. He was long-suffering. He was compassionate.

A thousand years hence no poet will think his literary career complete until he has written at least one poem dedicated to the Uncommon Commoner. No artist will feel that he is ready to lay down his brush until he has put upon canvas the dear, homely, beautiful face of Abraham Lincoln. No orator will believe himself ready to leave the public platform until he has woven into oratorical fabric his heart's tribute to the man who, born in a one-room log cabin lighted by a single window and with a dirt floor, climbed through pain, struggle, sacrifice and sorrow, to his place among the stars.

> A blend of mirth and sadness, of smiles and tears,
> A quaint knight errant of the pioneers;
> A homely hero, born of star and sod;
> A peasant prince: a masterpiece of God.

12

Jewels from King Solomon's Mines

And [Solomon] spake three thousand proverbs:
and his songs were a thousand and five.

1 KINGS 4:32

THERE is a popular legend that King Solomon secreted much of his vast treasure of jewels and gold in certain mines, and died without disclosing the location of the fabulous hidden wealth. The English writer, H. Rider Haggard, based his novel *King Solomon's Mines* on this legend, and the tale has recently been retold in the motion picture by that title. Happily, there are other mines of Israel's famous king which are not hidden but open to all who are of the mind to read the Biblical book of *Proverbs*. Here, in truth, are bright jewels of wisdom, which sparkle with epigrammatic brilliance and wit.

There is not a nation, a people, or a tribe without proverbs. The wisdom of the ages is in proverbial expressions, short, crisp sentences that tingle in the memory. There are said to be over ten thousand proverbs on the tongue alone, as, for instance, "Don't let your tongue cut off your head," and "A lengthy tongue, an early death." Taming the tongue, because of its difficulty, has inspired more proverbs than any other subject, and some of the cleverest of these have been produced by primitive peoples, for example, the natives of the Congo region in Africa.

Our everyday conversation is often interlarded with proverbs. They fall trippingly from off our lips; thus, "A bird in the hand is worth two in the bush," "A stitch in time saves nine," "Uneasy

lies the head that wears the crown," "Little pitchers have big
ears," "Birds of a feather flock together." The Sermon on the
Mount is brave with proverbial expressions, for example, "Ye
cannot serve God and mammon," "Give not that which is holy
unto the dogs, neither cast ye your pearls before swine," and
St. Paul is speaking in proverbs when he says, "Whatsoever a
man soweth that shall he also reap."

The proverb has been defined as "a statement of truth which
admits of general but not universal application." Some famous
proverbs contradict others equally famous, yet all of them contain at least a grain of truth. The French have a proverb which
says, "No general statement is true, not even this one." Here are
a few examples of proverbs that are contradictory: "Take care
of the pence and the pounds will take care of themselves." This
is excellent advice. Be thrifty, do not despise the day of small
things, yet, there is a danger that one will become so absorbed
with the trivialities of life, that he will lose the capacity to deal
with large affairs. Hence, we have the other proverb, "Penny
wise and pound foolish." Or, again, "Look before you leap."
Do not make hasty decisions. Think the matter through. There
is wisdom in this. Yet it is possible to look so long before you
leap that, when you are ready to leap, there isn't anything to
leap over—and the grand venture is lost. So we have the other
proverb, "He who hesitates is lost." There is truth in both. Take
another example, "Absence makes the heart grow fonder." So
it does—sometimes. Usually, we are more appreciated at home
after we have been absent for some time. Indeed, one of the joys
of leaving home is the anticipation of the welcome we may
receive when we return. But it is possible to stay away too long.
Thus, the other proverb, "Out of sight, out of mind."

The Book of Proverbs in the Holy Scriptures is one of the
most fascinating sections of the Old Testament. This book is
composite in character. Many of the proverbs in this collection
are attributed to Solomon, and in another book of the Bible
it is said that this famous king was the author of three thousand

proverbs. There are probably many authors represented in the portion designated as "The Proverbs." The sages of the long ago are represented in these maxims which have to do with conduct. They put a premium on integrity, exalt the homely virtues, show an almost uncanny insight into human nature, and some of them have a humorous twist.

I

"A word fitly spoken is like apples of gold in pictures of silver." Here is a pearl of wisdom. What a lovely phrase! A word fitly spoken is as beautiful and appealing as apples of gold in a silver-mounted frame, or, should you prefer, a "basket" of silver. Either phrasing will adequately translate the original. A word fitly spoken! What a witchery there is about words, and how we admire a lord of language. It was once my good fortune to become acquainted with a gentleman who as an explorer had lived many years in the Argentine. He told me that he was the first white man to penetrate some of the out-of-the-way sections of that country. He was an accomplished linguist, spoke ten languages, and understood several more. I asked him to differentiate for me the most important languages in his repertoire. He smiled as he replied, "If you wish to talk business, use English; if you are a diplomat, you should use French; if you want to call hogs, use German [my own opinion of German is much higher than this]; if you wish to make love, use Italian; and when you pray, use Spanish." He went on to tell me, then, that in those far stretches of the Argentine, sleeping out under the open sky, before he closed his eyes in sleep, he prayed to the Eternal in the Spanish tongue.

Now this is interesting, but I have a conviction that this English language of ours, which is composite and has been enriched by many other tongues, is quite adequate to talk business, manage diplomacy, make love, call hogs, and pray to the Heavenly Father. The poets have the gift to use fitly chosen words. For instance, here is an exquisite piece of versification by a com-

paratively unknown English lyric poet, Helen E. Holland.* It is
entitled "Waiting":

> Every day you do not come,
>   A little bit of summer dies,
> A rose leaf flutters from a rose
>   With less expectant eyes.
>
> Every day you do not come,
>   A blackbird from some lofty spray,
> Watches another sunset fade
>   And sings his soul away.
>
> Every day you do not come,
>   Some clinging tendril is untwined,
> The sweetness of the heliotrope
>   Is wasted on the wind.
>
> Every day you do not come,
>   A little later comes the dawn,
> A little sooner steals the dusk
>   Across the shadowed lawn.

Or, consider fitly spoken words when used by a lord of
speech, what music they make, what witchery is at the com-
mand of a great master of public speech. There are many
notable oratorical tributes to Abraham Lincoln. That of Colonel Henry Watterson, for example, with its dramatic climax;
and there also is Robert G. Ingersoll's eulogy of Lincoln, in
which occurs this perfect tribute, "He is the gentlest memory
of our world." Yet, the choicest piece of eloquence in the history of orations that have Abraham Lincoln for theme, as I
see it, was a brief tribute delivered by the late Homer Hoch,
Chief Justice of the Supreme Court of Kansas, in the national
House of Representatives, February 12, 1923. Here, indeed are
fitly spoken words of Corinthian eloquence:

There is no new thing to be said of Lincoln. There is no new
thing to be said of the mountains or of the sea or of the stars. The

* By courtesy of *The Poetry Review*, New York.

years go their way, but the same old mountains lift their granite shoulders above the drifting clouds; the same mysterious sea beats upon the shore; and the same silent stars keep holy vigil above a tired world. But to mountains and sea and stars men turn forever in unwearied homage. And thus with Lincoln. For he was mountain in grandeur of soul, he was sea in deep undervoice of mystic loneliness, he was star in steadfast purity of purpose and of service. And he abides.

"A word fitly spoken is like apples of gold in pictures of silver." To be sure, this proverb has a much wider application than that of the mastery of speech. It applies to human conduct. A word of admonition, rebuke, encouragement—such words may be spoken with an appropriateness meriting the highest praise. And to know when to speak the appropriate word, and how to speak it, the tone of the voice, the expression of the eyes, the lines about the mouth—how much is involved in this ministry of fitly spoken words!

D. L. Moody, famed evangelist, said that when as a youth he went to Chicago, where he became a shoe salesman, he was the loneliest of creatures. He longed for someone to greet him on the crowded street, saying, "Well, young fellow, it is good to meet you. How are you getting along?" And one day such a person met him, greeted him warmly and invited him to attend Sunday school and church. Moody's heart gave a joyous leap, and out of that chance meeting and a cheerful word came the young man's introduction to a glorious life of Christian activity. "A word fitly spoken is like apples of gold in pictures of silver."

II

"He that is slow to anger is better than the mighty; and he that ruleth his spirit than he that taketh a city." This is a flashing ruby of admonition. Here is a proverb that lauds self-control. No man can master others or a situation until he has learned to master himself. In my college days as a student at Transylvania, Lexington, Kentucky, I heard a lecture by Colonel

George W. Bane on the subject, "Characteristic Traits of the Masses." His thesis was that every section of America has its peculiarities of speech as well as other eccentricities. Colonel Bane said, "If you call a man a liar in Kentucky, he'll shoot you or knock you down." This statement was greeted with some applause in the rear of the chapel. "If you call a man a liar in Indiana, he will say, 'You are another,' but if you call a man a liar in the state of Maine, he'll say, 'Now you prove that.'" At this point Colonel Bane drew himself up to his full height, paused, and exclaimed, "Loyal Kentuckian that I am, I take off my hat to the man from Maine." The applause was thunderous.

Now there used to be a man in Maine whose name was on many tongues, the Honorable Thomas Brackett Reed. He was congressman and famous Speaker of the national House of Representatives, and was a formidable candidate for the nomination for President of the United States in 1896. He was a big man intellectually and also physically. He weighed above two hundred pounds and was huge of frame. He was a great "three decker" sort of man and as he walked along the street he had something of the swing of a sea captain who when on land still fancies he must respond to the roll of his ship. Mr. Reed was often sarcastic. I recall former Vice-President Adlai E. Stevenson of Bloomington, Illinois, relating this incident: Mr. Reed was in the Speaker's chair and Congressman Springer, a Democrat of Illinois, concluded a speech by quoting, dramatically, the words of Henry Clay: "I would rather be right than be President." At this juncture Speaker Reed leaned over his desk and drawled, "The gentleman from Illinois will never be either."

In the biography of Speaker Reed, written by Samuel W. McCall, a former Governor of Massachusetts, there is a charming anecdote of Mr. Reed and his little girl. It was in the Reed home in the Pine Tree State, and this little girl was curled up on a chair in the library when the door opened and her father came in. She looked up and saw that the favorite cat was sleeping soundly in her father's office chair and, sensing a possible debacle, she sprang from her chair, tripped across the floor, and attempted to spill the cat out of her father's chair and reset it for him, but in her haste and concern she pulled the chair clear out from under him. He sat down ponderously and got up painfully. His face was scarlet and for a second it looked as if anything might happen. Then that big man from Maine smiled, looked quizzically at his little girl and said, "My dear, I should like for you to know that it is much easier to get a new pussy than it is a new papa." "He that is slow to anger is better than the mighty; and he that ruleth his spirit than he that taketh a city."

Most anybody can lose his temper, but it takes a strong-minded man or woman to control it under great provocation. The scientists inform us that every time we lose our tempers, we release poisons in our bodies which destroy our ability or, at any rate, impair our capacity to make wise decisions. Who doubts it? Not I!

When I was a young minister, a physician whom I came to know quite intimately brought me a poem one Sunday morning and said, "I hope you memorize these lines and that you repeat them as long as you live." The author is Ella Wheeler Wilcox, but I do not recall having seen these stanzas in any of her published works which I have examined:

> I sometimes feel so passionate a yearning
> For spiritual perfection here below.
> This bodily frame, with healthful, fervent burning,
> Seems my determined foe.
>
> It interrupts my soul's intense devotions;
> Some hope it strangles of divinest birth;
> With a swift rush of violent emotions
> That link me to the earth.

It is as if two foes contended
    Within my bosom in deadly strife:
One for the loftier goals for souls intended,
    And one for earthly life.

And yet I know the very warfare within me
    Which brings out all my self-control,
Will in the end win for me
    The loved and longed-for goal.

The very fire which seems sometimes so cruel,
    Is the white light that shows me my own strength,
A furnace fed by the divinest fuel,
    It may become at length.

Ah, when within the immortal ranks enlisted,
    I sometimes wonder if we shall not find
That not by deeds but by what we have resisted,
    Our places are assigned.

III

The third proverb I present is like a sparkling diamond, and justly popular: "Where no vision is, the people perish." This is a truism but it will bear repetition. Without the dreams that inspired the glorious deed, there would have been no achievement. No book has been written, no canvas glorified, no building erected, no enterprise finished without the dream, the vision splendid. And the most fruitful time for dreaming is in the golden days of youth. We speak of the Pilgrim Fathers, but the Pilgrim Fathers were mostly young men. Of the 102 souls who came over on the Mayflower, the historians say that only seven were above fifty years of age. William Bradford, who became the second governor of the colony, was thirty-one; Edwin Winslow was twenty-six; and John Alden was twenty-one. There was quite a "mess" of children on board the Mayflower, and it will be remembered that Master Francis Millington fired off a fowling piece in the cabin of the Mayflower, with a keg of powder near by, uncovered. They had lively times on the

Mayflower because youth was there, venturesome, dreaming, audacious youth. Of the fifty-five men who framed the Constitution, the youngest was twenty-six, the oldest eighty-three, the average age, forty-three and a fraction.

"Where no vision is, the people perish." It is the year 1760, and the place is the colonial capital of Virginia, Williamsburg. I am interested in a young man that I see about the campus of William and Mary College. He is tall, slender, and his hair is reddish. His eyes shine with the light of a strange maturity. Nothing escapes his scrutiny. He loves to be in the company of such men as George Wythe, that famed Virginia lawyer at whose feet sat so many to learn the law and the reasons thereof; Doctor Small, professor of philosophy; and Governor Francis Fauquier, a man of the world and charming. From these men he learns the ways of the world and the wisdom that comes both from experience and from study. Later I see this young man in the legislature of Virginia, introducing five bills for human liberation, to wit: for the freedom of estates from the law of primogeniture; of property from the snarl of the laws of entailment; for the freedom of the slave; another for the freedom of the mind through the establishment of a public-school system; and lastly, a bill for the freedom of the soul, demanding the separation of Church and State. I behold this young man sitting down to write the Declaration of Independence before he was old enough to qualify for the Presidency. I see him Governor of Virginia; Minister to France; Secretary of State in George Washington's Cabinet; Vice-President in the John Adams administration; and then serving two terms as President of the United States.

Then at the close of these years in public position, this man, still dreaming, returns to his beloved home, Monticello, and proceeds to dream into existence the University of Virginia. The plan and program of this institution was his; he designed the main buildings, and through a telescope watched the structure go up, brick upon brick. He designed the curriculum, saw to it that there were no religious tests, yet welcomed to the campus every religious body and made opportunity that the spokesmen thereof might be heard. He was an inventive genius, this dreamer. He invented the riding plow, the flexible camp stool, the "Murphy bed," though he did not give it this name. He designed a folding ladder, and Monticello was full of gadgets that were born in this man's fertile brain. He was the greatest bookman of his day, and when adversity came upon him, sold his library for a little less than $25,000 to the Government, which was just about half what it cost him originally. He was an authority on Indian lore, a scientific farmer, a lord of language, and an expert in the science of government. In his old age, when his home was a Mecca for pilgrims from all over the world, he employed his time in writing maxims for his grandchildren. Here are a few of these maxims:

> Adore God.
> Love your neighbor as yourself, and your country more than
> yourself.
> No man regrets having eaten too little.*

At last the end came for this great old man who was still dreaming dreams and seeing visions. To those standing by his bedside he murmured, in the language of the Scriptures, "Now lettest Thy servant depart in peace." What a dreamer was Thomas Jefferson!

"Where no vision is, the people perish." It is the year 1850, and lo, a young woman, a schoolteacher, born of Quaker stock, decides to give up her teaching in order to become the advocate of an unpopular cause. She decides to give the rest of her life in behalf of her shackled sex. Certainly, it was a man's world which she looked out upon when she began her crusade. No

* I delivered this address at a Commencement of Denison University, Granville, Ohio. Mr. and Mrs. Henry Ford were present, a niece of Mrs. Ford being among the graduates. After the exercises were over Mr. Ford requested a copy of the address, saying, "That statement of Jefferson that 'No man regrets eating too little' just fits me." E. DeW. J.

married woman had any legal right to any money she might earn. A husband might give away his wife's children without any legal recourse on her part. One small college in the land opened its doors to women. Women could not vote upon any question. It was the day when women were wearing six petticoats at the same time, a symbol of the restricted life of American womanhood. When this woman began her reform, her audiences were small and hostile, but she went on undiscouraged. In truth, the opposition whetted her enthusiasm. She made a transcontinental tour, and by the time she reached California, the size of her audiences had multiplied many times. A few years passed and her fame spread abroad. She was classed with such princes of the platform as Henry Ward Beecher, Wendell Phillips, and John B. Gough. She went to England, and was a guest of Queen Victoria. She spoke to thousands who crowded the largest halls available. She did not live to see the coming of universal suffrage in America, but she lived long enough to find a shrine in the hearts of the people. How familiar to the public were her strong features, clean-cut profile, hair parted in the middle and smoothed back over her ears, a black silk dress with delicate ruching about her neck, bright eyes gleaming from behind gold-rimmed spectacles. What a dreamer was Susan B. Anthony!

IV

"Seest thou a man wise in his own conceit? there is more hope of a fool than of him." Here is an opal of admonition. He is a wise man who knows that he does not know it all. There have been some great men who were conceited, but they would have been greater without this handicap. "Let no man think more highly of himself than he ought to think," is one of St. Paul's wisest admonitions. Colossal conceit is not without its humorous aspect. There was Joseph Parker, that famed preacher, who built the City Temple and made it the Cathedral of Nonconformity in London. Dr. Parker did not lie awake at night hating himself. Many are the stories told of his weakness in this respect. Once, it is told, he went into his pulpit, looked out over his audience of two thousand persons, pressed his hands to his temples, and exclaimed, "This great brain is tired." On another occasion, a young preacher in a village church wrote to Dr. Parker asking him to come out on some week night and lecture or preach in the little church to which he ministered. Parker did not so much as take the trouble to use a fresh sheet of paper, but wrote at the bottom of the young man's letter as follows: "How can the eagle sit in the sparrow's nest?" I want to believe that Dr. Parker sent the young preacher a second letter saying he would be delighted to come and preach for him. Here was a preacher who was great despite this eccentricity, certainly not because of it.

There are many stories told of Henry Ward Beecher. Some of them are apocryphal, and it is difficult sometimes to separate the true from the false. Here is one that may well be true. Beecher was on a lecture tour in the Middle West, and was marooned in a little Indiana town, because of a wreck ahead of the train on which he was riding. Finding himself obliged to spend the night in this village, the Brooklyn preacher learned that there was a revival in progress. He hunted up the church and, as he passed through the door, the young preacher, who was a little "cocky," was just beginning his sermon. Now, there was no more familiar figure among the public men of that day than that of Henry Ward Beecher: the long hair curling over his coat collar, the flashing eyes, the mobile lips, the stocky form. Almost everybody recognized readily this Shakespeare of the pulpit. Certainly this young preacher must have identified his distinguished visitor at once, but instead of saying to the congregation, "I see Henry Ward Beecher is in this audience. I don't know what miracle brought him here, but I know that I speak for you all when I say, 'Mr. Beecher, come into the pulpit and preach for us' "—instead of doing this, this ministerial fledgling went on with his sermon and possibly put in a few extras for Mr. Beecher.

After the sermon had been preached and the benediction pronounced, the young parson hurried back to the door, where Mr. Beecher was surrounded by a group of people shaking hands with him and plying him with questions, introduced himself, and said: "Mr. Beecher, I am proud to have had you in my audience tonight. I don't know how it happened, but it is wonderful to have you here. Did you get anything out of my sermon?" "I did," he replied. Whereupon, the young fellow, still prodding for praise and quite unconscious of what was about to occur, queried, "Mr. Beecher, I wish you would tell me just how my sermon helped you." The famous preacher's eyes twinkled. "I am glad to do so. Three weeks ago I heard Phillips Brooks preach, and it was so powerful a sermon I went away vowing that I would never go into the pulpit again, but since I have heard you, I have changed my mind." "Seest thou a man wise in his own conceit? there is more hope of a fool than of him."

The open mind is desirable. The humblest learner is the ideal student. The most profound scholars are ever aware of their limitations. Conceit is an enemy of humility. Arrogance makes it difficult for sincerity to come into its own. It was said of a conceited American statesman "that he strutted sitting down." If so, one naturally wonders what this celebrity did *standing up!*

V

"Keep thy heart with all diligence; for out of it are the issues of life." Surely this proverb is a sapphire of rare beauty. There are more than a thousand references in the Bible to the heart. In some places, the intellect is meant, as in the Scripture, "Why reason you these things in your heart?" In other references, the will faculty is in the mind of the writer, thus, "Let each man do according as he hath purposed in his heart." In the great sweep of the Biblical use of the word heart, the whole man is meant, with the affections as the ruling quality. This is as it should be. Horace Bushnell once said that unless a man lives in his heart, he does not live at all. To live in the affections is to live in "A house by the side of the road, where the sons of men pass by." To live in the affections is not merely to "live and let live," but rather to "live and help live."

Some years ago I ran across a humorous episode in a comic paper. It was a scene in an American home. Supper was over, the man of the house was reading his newspaper, and his young son, who was getting along fairly well in his school studies, asked his father some pertinent questions: "Father, what is charity?" Father laid down his paper, "Charity, my boy, is giving away something you don't want." "But Father, what is Organized Charity?" "Organized Charity, my son, is giving away something you do not want, to somebody who does not want it, who will give it to somebody else who will lose it." . . . "Well then, Father, what is love?" "Love! Why, love is sharing something you would like to keep with somebody who needs it more than you do, but I would have you know, boy, that love is mighty expensive; it costs a heap."

Yes, love is costly. It has always been so. If a man love a woman, or a woman love a man, or a human being love a mighty cause, these loves call for sacrifice, for toil and tears, and it may be life itself. It is good to recall the words of the greatest of the apostles and what he wrote to a group of men and women who were beguiled by the so-called "gift of tongues," "If I speak with the tongues of men and of angels, but have not love, I am become sounding brass, or a clanging cymbal. . . . And if I bestow all my goods to feed the poor, and if I give my body to be burned, but have not love, it profiteth me nothing. . . . Love suffereth long, and is kind . . . beareth all things, believeth all things, hopeth all things, endureth all things. . . . But now abideth faith, hope, love, these three, and the greatest of these is love" (ASV). "Keep thy heart with all diligence; for out of it are the issues of life."

Once in a lifetime, perhaps, there happens to us something so unusual and of such a nature that we can never quite forget it. It has a way of appearing and reappearing in our dreams by day and night; and at length it becomes part and parcel of our very being. This incident I am about to relate happened in Bloomington, Illinois, my residence for many years. In that sprightly city of the Corn Belt, I once knew a Negro who was the headwaiter in the Illinois Hotel. He was a man of good personality and high ideals, and fairly well educated. He and his wife were building a home and rearing a family, against heavy odds. At the time of which I speak, they had a little girl named Nellie, about eight years of age, and remarkably gifted in recitations and dramatic reading. To be specific, it was the year 1919, and Madame Sarah Bernhardt was on a farewell tour from coast to coast. The local theater had announced this famous actress for a one-night performance, and a week before she appeared in Bloomington, I met my friend the headwaiter on the Courthouse Square. He greeted me warmly.

"Doctor," he said, "would you do me a favor?" "Well, that depends," I replied. "Tell me what you have in mind." "Well, sir, you must know that this Madame Bernhardt is to give a play here in a few days." "Yes, what of it?" I rejoined. "Doctor, would you do me the great favor of writing to this great actress and asking her if she would kindly hear our little girl Nellie recite?" This seemed to me to be a pretty large order, and my face must have reflected my feelings, for my friend the headwaiter proceeded to press his case with increased vigor. "Doctor, this would mean everything to us, if Madame Bernhardt would hear our little girl. If you will just write the letter, even if nothing comes of it, I'll be ever so grateful." I promised to write the letter, admonishing my friend not to be disappointed if nothing came of it. A few hours later I wrote the following letter:

Dear Madame Bernhardt: I hope you will pardon an entire stranger thus addressing you, but we have in this city a very worthy Negro family whose little girl is wonderfully gifted in dramatic recitations. Now, these good people have dreamed a great dream of your hearing their little girl recite. If you could possibly grant them the privilege of an interview and complied with their request, it would be a red-letter day in their humble home, and they would never forget your kindness as long as they live.

I signed my name to this letter and sent it to the manager of the local theater; then I left town, for a speaking date. I was not in Bloomington when Madame Bernhardt gave her performance but down in Southern Illinois speaking at a teachers' institute. Two days later, I returned, and one of the first men that I met as I got off the streetcar at the Public Square was my friend the headwaiter. His face was beaming. "Doctor, have you heard the news?" I said, "No," and he continued, his face aglow: "Doctor, Madame Bernhardt heard Nellie. It was the most wonderful thing that ever happened to us. She had my wife and me and the little girl come to her private car. Doctor, were you ever in Madame Bernhardt's private car?" I assured him that I had never had that experience. "Well, sir, that car was fixed up like a room in a house; rugs on the floor, pictures on the wall, and a piano in one corner. I never knew that private cars were fixed up like that. Well, now, Madame Bernhardt heard the little girl recite three pieces, and then she called Nellie over to her, put her hand on the little girl's head, and said (she spoke through an interpreter), 'Nellie, you have the gift; but take it from one who has been on the stage for a long time, there is something else for a woman to do besides entertaining the public. Don't let this turn your head. You have the gift, but don't let it spoil you.' Then she turned to me and my wife, and gave us the same advice about the little girl. 'Keep her back; keep her back. Don't spoil her.' That's what she said. Then, Doctor, she took three long-stemmed roses from a tall vase that was on the table at her side and gave them to Nellie. We are going to keep the roses till the petals fall. Then we will press them between the pages of the Big Book."

As the headwaiter gave me this account of the meeting in Madame Bernhardt's private car, the glow on his face deepened and his eyes filled with tears. I, too, was stirred by the story, and wondered if Madame Bernhardt in all her life had done anything more beautiful than this gracious kindness done for my headwaiter friend and his wife and little girl. And when death came to Bernhardt in Paris, and the newspapers of the world were giving her columns of tribute, I wrote an editorial for the Detroit *News* entitled "The Passing of Sarah Bernhardt," and as I composed the editorial there came between me and the typewritten page the memory of this incident that happened at Bloomington; and I seemed to see again the glowing face and misty eyes of the headwaiter as he told me of this modern instance of keeping the heart with all diligence.

Robert Burns shall have the closing words:

> . . . how poor Religion's pride,
>   In all the pomp of method, and of art,
> When men display to congregations wide,
>   Devotion's every grace, except the heart!
> The Power, incensed, the pageant will desert,
> The pompous strain, the sacerdotal stole;
>   But haply, in some cottage far apart,
> May hear, well pleased, the language of the soul;
> And in his Book of Life the inmates poor enroll.

And these lines, from an epistle of Burns to a brother poet:

> If happiness hae not her seat
>   And center in the breast,
> We may be wise, or rich, or great,
>   But never can be blest:
>   Nae treasures, nor pleasures
>   Could make us happy lang;
>   The heart ay's the part ay,
>   That makes us right or wrang.

13

A Magnificent Obsession

Brethren, I count not myself to have apprehended: but this one thing I do, forgetting those things which are behind, and reaching forth unto those things which are before, I press toward the mark for the prize of the high calling of God in Christ Jesus.

PHILIPPIANS 3:13, 14

THESE are the thrilling words of the apostle Paul, who, next to Jesus Christ himself, is the greatest of all the illustrious characters of the Bible. He was born a Jew, a Pharisee of the Pharisees, a member of the strictest of the Jewish sects of his day. Educated at the feet of the learned Gamaliel, he soon became a leader among the prominent young rabbis of his day. At an early age he began to exhibit the hostility of his sect toward the followers of Christ, persecuted and harried them, boldly seizing and committing them to prison. He was present at the stoning of Stephen, consented to his death, and the garments of the executioners were laid at his feet.

It was while he was on his way to Damascus, bent, no doubt, on a bloody mission, that his conversion took place. Jesus Christ appeared to him in a burst of surpassing glory, and he heard a voice saying to him, "Saul, Saul, why persecutest thou me." And from the depths of his sad heart he replied: "What shall I do, Lord?" And when he was shown his duty he set about his mission with incredible zeal.

Commissioned to preach the gospel to the Gentiles, he who had been Saul the Rabbi became Paul, an apostle of Jesus Christ. The choice was a wise one, since most of his fellow apostles were fishermen, unlearned yet loyal, stouthearted men. Here was a man fitted by nature and training to stand before kings and queens and the pedantic philosophers of his day, and preach with persuasive eloquence, Jesus Christ and Him crucified.

From this apostle's lips fell some of the most rapt flights of eloquence ever uttered by mortal man. He stood in chains before King Agrippa and Queen Bernice, and amid the pomp and ceremony of that dissolute court, this man, by the grace of God, made a noble and impassioned defense of his newly found faith, a classic of its kind, and destined to be chronicled among the celebrated speeches of all times.

Talk about persecution! This Herald of the Good News about Jesus Christ wrote:

Of the Jews five times received I forty stripes save one. Thrice was I beaten with rods, once was I stoned, thrice I suffered shipwreck, a night and a day have I been in the deep; in journeyings often, in perils of rivers, in perils of robbers, in perils from my countrymen, in perils from the Gentiles, in perils in the city, in perils in the wilderness, in perils in the sea, in perils among false brethren; in labor and travail, in watchings often, in hunger and thirst, in fastings often, in cold and nakedness [ASV].

Lied about, betrayed, slandered, imprisoned, yet faltering never, and saying, "I have learned in whatsoever state I am, therein to be content."

And yet, this heroic soul, this spiritual giant, greatest of the apostolic company, in writing to the church at Philippi, said: "Brethren, I count not myself to have apprehended." Now there is a nice distinction between the words "apprehend" and "comprehend." To apprehend means to seize, to grasp, to know in part; comprehend means to understand, to know more fully. The very idea of God presupposes that He may be apprehended but not comprehended by rational beings. We may say that we apprehend something of the character of Marcus Brutus as Shakespeare delineates him in his tragedy of Julius Caesar, but who would be so brash as to claim he *comprehended* all the myriad-minded poet meant to convey in creating that noble but frustrated Roman who spoke so feelingly of "the ruddy drops that visit my sad heart."

What did Paul mean by the words "I count not myself to have apprehended"? The answer is, I conjecture, that he had not yet entered fully into the mystery of the Eternal God as revealed in Jesus Christ; of the ineffable love, grace and truth made manifest, wherein the Word became flesh; of the "terrible beauty of the cross," counting himself but a child in the school of Christ, a learner in that school until the end of his God-intoxicated mission.

The greatest of earth are usually the humblest. Sir Isaac Newton, toward the close of his life, likened himself to a child picking up pebbles on the seashore, while the vast ocean of undiscovered truths swept out and away from him. Humboldt, old, and come to the time of sunset and evening star, cried, "O that I had another century to live. I have just begun to learn." What preacher of parts was ever wholly satisfied with the best of his preaching? How little we know of what is yet to be known. Who coined the phrase, "The unsearchable riches of Christ"? Who spoke of himself as the least of the apostles? Why, the same Great-heart who said "I count not myself to have apprehended"!

"But this one thing I do." "*One thing* I do"; not five thousand things I dabble at. "One thing I do"; not myriad things I toy with. One thing I *do,* not merely dream of doing. "One thing I do." Detach this phrase from the rest of the sentence and it could serve admirably as a motto for innumerable graduating classes. Singleness of purpose, definite aims—how basic these are in life! Most persons have but one good fight within their power; the exceptional person may have the capacity for two hard fights; few have the will and wit for three. Versatility has charms, and also perils. Too many irons in the fire may deaden

the flame. How easy it is to be a "Jack of all trades and master of none."

In my Kentucky days as a young preacher I ordained to the ministry a young man in the congregation who gave much promise. He was bright, enthusiastic, and industrious. I had vast hopes for him. He took a church and was off to a good start. Presently, he bought a farm and stocked it; next he ran for County Superintendent of Schools and was elected. Then he tried out as an auctioneer; and later studied law and was admitted to the bar. All the time he kept on preaching, looking at first upon these various activities as secondary in importance. Eventually, however, these so-called "side issues" became his chief concern, and his ministry took a beating from which it never recovered. "One thing I do," not this thing, and that thing, and still another thing, and miss the main thing.

"Forgetting the things which are behind." Few of us have the will or the courage to forget. Henry Ward Beecher believed that next to a good memory is a good forgettery. Brooding over the things behind disturbs and unfits us for life at its best. How well the apostle knew this. Suppose he had permitted himself to brood over his participation in Stephen's death, seeming again to see that youthful martyr who died with a prayer for his executioners on his lips; and in imagination hear again the sickening thud of stones as they crushed out the life of one who so richly deserved to live. But no, the apostle would not let the memory of that bloodstained past put hobbles on his one increasing purpose. So, he willed to forget the things that were behind, being not disobedient to the heavenly vision.

Then, too, it is possible to linger lovingly on the triumphs of the past to one's hurt. When a minister has preached a better sermon, a craftsman turned out a better job, a writer produced a better book, there is often present the disposition to rest upon the success of yesterday to the hurt of the workmanship of today and the tomorrows.

There is a striking story which is pertinent here. Once there was a famous painter who had a pupil of great promise, who, while still in his apprentice years, painted a remarkably fine picture. So elated was he with this achievement that he put aside his palette, laid down his brushes, and spent his time mooning over his picture, rounding up his friends to join him in admiring his handiwork. The master observed this conduct of his gifted pupil with concern, and one morning he went to the studio early, and dipping a large brush in black paint he swiftly smeared the canvas with huge daubs, and thus ruined the painting. When his pupil arrived at the studio and saw what had happened, he became hysterical, tore at his hair, sobbed and wailed. The master painter stood by, a silent and sympathetic observer of his pupil's grief, and when the storm had passed, the master spoke: "I did it for your own good; you have greater pictures within your soul, but you will never put them on canvas as long as you are satisfied with this one." Now it came about that this young artist later painted a picture known as "The Sacrifice of Iphigenia," a canvas which found a place in one of the famous galleries of Europe. The apostle knew whereof he reasoned. It is common sense to forget both success and failure, and hail the future with a cheer!

"Reaching forth unto those things which are before, I press on." The things that await our doing, the open doors that invite us to enter, the acceptance of new responsibilities, the call to new departures—Oh, the glory of going on! What were the "things before" that were in the apostle's mind? Well, always his mission; new converts to win for Christ, new churches to be established, new friends in Christ to make, and hold most dear. Yes, and new privations for Christ's sake; new enemies of the stumbling block of the cross. And, besides these, his concern for all the churches. It was an exciting life this missionary to the Gentiles lived. It was anything but dull.

"The things before." Could it not be he had in mind also "the last things"? It could. He had written and spoken about "The

house not made with hands, eternal in the heavens." He had taught that death shall not be able to separate us from the love of God which is in Christ our Lord, and in this same Philippian letter he wrote that he was in a strait betwixt the two, having the desire to depart, and be with Christ, which was far better for him, or, to abide in the flesh, which was better for his dear friends at Philippi. Intimations of immortality, soon or late, come to all of us, and especially to the pure in heart. How unforgettably Wordsworth put it:

> Hence in a season of calm weather
> Though inland far we be,
> Our Souls have sight of that immortal sea
> Which brought us hither,
> Can in a moment travel thither,
> And see the Children sport upon the shore,
> And hear the mighty waters rolling evermore.

"*I press on.*" There is a story of an early missionary to the American Indians, in which a convert, in his elation, set about to write a Christian hymn. He gave it his best, and on completing his masterpiece, proudly brought it to the missionary in charge. Translated, the chorus ran like this:

> Go on! Go on! Go on! Go on!
> Go on! Go on! Go on! Go on!
> Go on! Go on! Go on! Go on!
> Go on! Go on! Go on! Go on!

A crude attempt at writing a hymn, I concede, but the sentiment is in perfect harmony with the ringing words "forgetting those things which are behind and reaching forth unto those things which are before, *I press on.*" J. G. Holland phrased it succinctly,

> Heaven is not reached at a single bound:
> But we build the ladder by which we rise
> From the lowly earth to the vaulted skies,
> And we mount to its summit round by round.

How vividly I recall a long-cherished day when, with a companion who knew intimately trees, birds and flowers, we inspected a giant oak that had met disaster in a frightful storm. My friend carefully counted the rings on the end of a log sawed from the trunk of the tree, and announced the oak was two hundred and fifty years old. Then he called my attention to a strange scar which ran halfway across the heart of the sawed-off end of the log. "Sometime in the first fifty years of its long life," he explained, "this tree was injured; it is likely that another tree was driven against it with such violence as to mar this tree permanently, but the injury did not stunt its growth, so strong and sturdy it became, as it battled with storms, snow and ice for two and a half centuries."

I took to heart the lesson and tucked it away in memory for future use. Here, as I wrestle with this bugle blast of a text, I employ it gratefully. The apostle Paul bore the honorable scars of struggle and strife as he *pressed on*, and in a letter he wrote to the Galatian Christians he said: "Henceforth let no man trouble me; for I bear branded on my body the marks of Jesus." Magnificent obsession, indeed!

II

Three things at least, should be said of this man who was under the spell of a magnificent obsession. In the first place, he knew *where* he was going and never once lost his direction. This is much; yea, it is everything. So many people are like rudderless ships at sea. They have no sense of mission, no shining goal, but drift through life aimlessly, tragically. "Drifting with the tide" may be appropriate as a title for a ballad, but it wouldn't fit as a description of a first-century Christian. "Whither goest thou, Paul?" The answer: "I must see Rome at any cost!"

For a second thing, he knew *why* he was going. He gave reasons for the hope that was within him. He knew Him in whom he believed. It is not enough to believe a thing just because father stood for it, or mother cherished it. This is good if what they stood for was good, but it falls short of the best. "Study to shew thyself approved unto God, a workman that needeth not to be ashamed, rightly dividing the word of truth." So Paul wrote to Timothy. When I was a young preacher, one of my hosts used to quiz me in order to learn how well informed I was in the doctrines most commonly believed among us. As a guest in that house I used to dread this ordeal of questioning. Now I know it was good discipline for me. It put me on my mettle.

For a third thing, Paul wanted to take everybody with him along the way he was going. No spiritual isolationist was this apostle. Like Job, he could not eat his morsel *alone*. This is the man who, speaking in chains before King Herod Agrippa and his dissolute court, cried: "I would to God, that whether with little or with much, not thou only, but also all that hear me this day, might become such as I am, except these bonds." This is the missionary passion, the veritable lifeblood of Christianity.

"Press on!" Aye, that's the password. Paul is going God's way, which is forward, ever forward. Nor will the going be easy. There were great and effectual doors open, but the adversaries were numerous and fierce. To "press on" in the Godward course is to grow in the grace and knowledge of God in Christ, with horizons expanding and the light streaming along the path which shineth more and more unto the perfect day. Paul the apostle never stopped growing, a learner to the day he was bidden to "come up higher." In this letter to the Philippians he tells his dear friends how to grow in favor with God and man:

Finally, brethren, whatsoever things are true, whatsoever things are honorable, whatsoever things are just, whatsoever things are pure, whatsoever things are lovely, whatsoever things are of good report; if there be any virtue, and if there be any praise, think on these things [ASV].

III

This letter of the apostle Paul to the Philippians is one of his "prison epistles," and the dark shadows of the end were falling across the parchment as he dictated this love letter to the church at Philippi. Not long after he wrote to the Philippian Christians, he dictated the last letter of which we have any record, and, characteristically, that letter was addressed to Timothy, his son in the gospel:

I charge thee in the sight of God, and of Christ Jesus, who shall judge the living and the dead, and by his appearing and his kingdom; preach the word; be urgent in season, out of season; reprove, rebuke, exhort, with all longsuffering and teaching. For the time will come when they will not endure the sound doctrine; but, having itching ears, will heap to themselves teachers after their own lusts; and will turn away their ears from the truth, and turn aside unto fables. But be thou sober in all things, suffer hardship, do the work of an evangelist, fulfil thy ministry. For I am already being offered, and the time of my departure is come. I have fought the good fight, I have finished the course, I have kept the faith: henceforth there is laid up for me the crown of righteousness, which the Lord, the righteous judge, shall give to me at that day; and not to me only, but also to all them that have loved his appearing [ASV].

One scene more. It is the last. Under what specific charge the apostle Paul was put to death we do not know. It was enough for the Emperor to know that he was a leader of the "pernicious sect called Christians." The day came when Roman soldiers led him forth to die. Little they knew that they were taking to his coronation the battle-scarred veteran of a thousand spiritual conflicts. Overhead the bluest of skies, and the breezes that caressed his checks were balmy.

The place of the execution was reached, and this "prisoner of the Lord" obediently pillowed his head upon the block; the ax fell, and the hand that wrote "living oracles" was pulseless, and the tongue which had preached so eloquently Jesus Christ and

Him crucified, was silent. But not forever. For, in the sublime imagery of the Apocalypse, when that unnumbered host of the redeemed shall take up the strains of that new song of Moses and the Lamb, no tongue will move in sweeter harmony, or gladder accord, than that of him who, writing to the Saints at Philippi, said:

Brethren, I count not myself to have apprehended: but this one thing I do, forgetting those things which are behind, and reaching forth unto those things which are before, I press toward the mark for the prize of the high calling of God in Christ Jesus.

> So be my passing!
> My task accomplished and the long day done,
> My wages taken, and in my heart
> Some late lark singing,
> Let me be gathered to the quiet west,
> The sundown splendid and serene.*

* William E. Henley.

14

An American Apostle
of Brotherhood

Blessed are the peacemakers; for they shall be called sons of God.
JESUS

His heart was as great as the world but there was no room in it to
hold the memory of a wrong.   RALPH WALDO EMERSON

He is the gentlest memory of our world. ROBERT G. INGERSOLL

ALMOST any way we look at him, Abraham Lincoln was
a brotherly man. On one count, he was remarkably free
from petty prejudices; on another, his sense of humor and of
kindness saved him from returning in kind the ugly epithets
flung at him by fanatical contemporaries who goaded him un-
mercifully. The "prairie lawyer," as Vachel Lindsay called him,
was given to listening to "the still sad music of humanity," and
no other occupant of the "Executive Mansion," as Lincoln
dubbed it, was a better exponent of the credo that "a man's a
man for a' that"—a poem, by the way, he dearly loved.

To be brotherly is to be kind, is to be considerate, is to be just,
is to possess an understanding heart. Lincoln was all of these
grand qualities and he was more. Whether he inherited or
achieved these graces no one can say. Perhaps both are blended
in the portrait of his complex personality. We know but little
of his mother, and not a great deal about his father. What we
do know of Nancy Hanks Lincoln is that she was gentle and of
an affectionate nature. Of his father we glean from fragmentary
sources that in a rough way Thomas Lincoln was a well-disposed
pioneer, illiterate but not unintelligent, and quite able to live
on good terms with his neighbors.

This we do know: Young Abraham was never a trouble-maker, but always eager to make friends, not enemies. He had a well-established reputation early in life as a defender of the "underdog," revealed a kindness for dumb animals, and was without the lust to kill that was so common among the pioneers who believed they must conquer by force the wild wilderness way. This brotherly nature of Lincoln was ever in evidence throughout the Indiana and early Illinois years. So was this youth father to the man!

"When people talked of Lincoln," writes Carl Sandburg, "it was nearly always about one or more of these four things: (1) how long, tall, quick, strong or awkward he looked; (2) how he told stories and jokes; how he was comical, or pleasant, or kindly; (3) how he could be silent, melancholy, sad; (4) how he was ready to help a friend, a stranger or even a dumb animal in distress."

I

The acid test of a man's nature is the measure of his conduct in his home, among his children and with his wife. Lincoln met this severe test nobly and with a patience sublime. He was all tenderness with his high-spirited Mary and only in rare and exceptional cases did he chide or rebuke her. In so doing he was the greater sufferer of the two. His restraint on such occasions was marked with a deft considerateness.

He was never the martinet in his home; quite to the contrary, he treated his lively little boys, Willie and Tad, with an indulgence that sometimes startled and more often amused his secretaries. He endured the pranks of these lads with good-natured tolerance, even when they played hob with his inkstands and scattered important papers in profusion on the floor of the office.

As a family man Abraham Lincoln was all that a husband and father should be, with a noteworthy leaning to the side of gentleness and a vast forgiveness. I agree with Dr. William E. Barton, noted biographer, in this appraisement:

Mary Lincoln loved her husband. If she had not loved him there was no need of her marrying him, for many men sought her hand when she was at liberty to choose among the most brilliant men of Springfield. While he offended her by his lack of polish and his ignorance of social usage, he still realized in large measure her ambitious dreams of what her husband might be and the position to which his success would and did evidently elevate her. Marriage is a school of discipline, and its lessons often hard and exacting for both husband and wife, and this the Lincolns knew full well.

II

War tests men, and women likewise, to the marrow of their souls. It vexes men's judgments and distorts their vision so that they become myopic and often blind to truth, justice and mercy. During the fierce war years, Lincoln never once made a speech or wrote a letter in which the poison of hate entered or corroding partisanship pervaded. He never denounced the enemy in scurrilous terms or waved the "bloody shirt." It was simply not in him to do this, although others could and did this rattling of the sword and the calling of vile names. He could be firm and speak or write in majestic indignation with the fire and fury of the ancient prophets. But even then his diction was lofty and he dealt with principles rather than personalities.

Oftener he was "slow to smite and swift to spare." Thus he could say and mean it, "I have not only suffered by the South: I have suffered with the South." That suffering was written on his furrowed face and discernible in the tones of his voice. He too, like the Saviour of men, was a man of sorrows and acquainted with grief. Only those who themselves have suffered can successfully comfort others who journey through the valley of the shadow. Lincoln's letter to the Widow Bixby is known the world over; the letter which follows, written to Miss Fanny

McCullough of Bloomington, Illinois, deserves to be more widely known than it is:

Executive Mansion, Washington,
December 23, 1862.

Dear Fanny: It is with deep grief that I learn of the death of your kind and brave father; and, especially, that it is affecting your young heart beyond what is common in such cases. In this sad world of ours, sorrow comes to all; and to the young it comes with bitterest agony, because it takes them unawares. The older have learned to ever expect it. I am anxious to afford some alleviation of your present distress. Perhaps relief is not possible, except with time. You cannot now realize that you will ever feel better. Is not this so? And yet it is a mistake. You are sure to be happy again. To know this, which is certain to be true, will make you less miserable now. I have had experience enough to know what I say; and you need only to believe it, to feel better at once. The memory of your dear father, instead of an agony, will yet be a sad sweet feeling in your heart, of a purer and holier sort than you have yet known before.

Please present my kind regards to your afflicted mother.

Your sincere friend,
A. Lincoln

War with all its attendant bitterness could not harden the compassionate heart of Abraham Lincoln.

Once when the dreadful conflict was at its zenith, partisanship rampant, and emotions drenched with hate, a revealing incident took place at the White House. A reception was on and the President spoke hopefully, kindly, about the South. Instantly an elderly woman indignantly asked him how he could speak in such a manner of the enemy, and he replied ever so gently: "What, Madam? Do I not destroy them when I make them my friends?" There is no answer to such wise speech. No man in public life throughout our long history knew so well or practiced more perfectly the fine art of unmaking enemies than did Abraham Lincoln.

III

Prejudice tests men, tests them sorely; prejudice of race, and creed, and class. Prejudice, intolerance and ill will are long-time foes of brotherhood. How grandly Lincoln rose above both the petty and the base prejudices that ride human beings like "The Old Man of the Sea"! Look at the shining record and rejoice in one so free from this blight as was the man who led the nation through four purgatorial years of war without hate in his heart.

Along about 1853 and continuing for several years, a secret political party emerged in the United States, the object of which was to render politically powerless, through stringent legislation, those other than native Americans. It was popularly known as the "Know-Nothing" party—so named because when asked about it the members replied, "I don't know." This party was a forerunner of The American Protection Association, popularly known as the A.P.A. and, later, the movement known as the Ku Klux Klan. In each instance many good citizens mistakenly aligned themselves with these organizations only to regret it later, as the movements ran amok, and did vast harm.

Abraham Lincoln's opinion of the Know-Nothing party and similar movements was stated in a letter which he wrote to his intimate friend, Joshua F. Speed, under date of August 24, 1855. He said:

I am not a Know-Nothing, that is certain. How could I be? How can anyone who abhors the oppression of Negroes be in favor of degrading classes of white people? Our progress in degeneracy appears to me to be pretty rapid. As a nation we began by declaring that "all men are created equal." We now practically read it "all men are created equal, except Negroes." When the Know-Nothings get control, it will read: "All men are created equal, except Negroes and foreigners and Catholics." When it comes to this, I shall prefer emigrating to some country where they make no pretense of loving liberty—to Russia, for instance, where despotism can be taken pure and without the base alloy of hypocrisy.

Abraham Lincoln was the first President to offer a Jew an appointment as a full-fledged minister to a foreign power, the post of minister to Italy having been offered to Sigismund Kaufman of New York, but rejected by him.

Mr. Lincoln appointed a Jew by the name of Einstein United States consul to Nuremberg, Germany, destined to be in time the world capital of anti-Semitism. It was Lincoln's policy when he found an honest and competent man to invest with responsibility, not to inquire as to his race or creed.

Lincoln was the first President to appoint a Jewish army chaplain, Dr. Arnold Fischel of New York getting the appointment in 1862, after Congress passed special legislation making it legal.

When General Grant, in 1863, promulgated an order excluding all Jews from his department, the President promptly revoked it. Such an act was alien to his nature.

IV

It is said that when Arthur, Duke of Wellington, surveyed the battlefield of Waterloo after his triumph there, he sadly remarked: "Next to a great defeat the saddest thing in all the world is a great victory." Whether Lincoln was acquainted with this wise saying of history we do not know; anyhow, he knew the truth of the observation and planned to manage the victory over the South with compassion and justice. He loved to think of the recreant states as part of the one big family which had wandered away from home, and he planned to welcome them back and help them to set about keeping house again. No, he would not kill the fatted calf or put a ring on their fingers, but he would, God helping him, destroy the spirit of hate and vengeance which he knew rankled in the hearts of many.

There is a scene in Drinkwater's play, *Abraham Lincoln,* that is not easy to describe in speech or do justice to on paper. The President is alone in his office. He goes over to a wall map and stands before it—a map of the United States. Suddenly he lifts his long arms in a gesture of embrace, as if he sought to draw to his bosom the reunited country—all—all of the states—back home again, and to stay!*

When the news came of the surrender of General Lee's Army of Virginia near Appomattox, President Lincoln received it, not with exultation, but with a deep, quiet sense of relief and a vast thankfulness. The great hour had come and he was ready to meet it in a spirit of conciliation. Gideon Welles, Secretary of the Navy in the Lincoln cabinet, in a magazine article gave a vivid description of the meeting of the President's official family, which took place on the morning of the fatal 14th of April, 1865. Reconstruction of the Southern states was the principal subject for discussion, and a tone of severity was in the speech of some. Secretary Welles reported the President as saying:

I think it providential that this great rebellion is crushed just as Congress has adjourned and there are none of the disturbing elements of that body to hinder and embarrass us. If we are wise and discreet we shall reanimate the states and their governments in successful operation, with order prevailing and the Union reëstablished before Congress comes together in December. . . .

I hope there will be no persecution, no bloody work after the war is over. No one need expect me to take any part in hanging or killing those men, even the worst of them.

Frighten them out of the country, open the gates, let down the bars, scare them off—[throwing up his hands as if scaring sheep]—enough lives have been sacrificed!

We must extinguish our resentments if we expect harmony and reunion. There is too much of a desire on the part of some of our very good friends to be masters, to interfere with and dictate to

---

* This incident in substance appears in Chap. 8, and is used again because of its pertinency.

those states, to treat the people not as fellow-citizens; there is too little respect for their rights.

Thus spoke the Apostle of Brotherhood, whose sane and spacious statesmanship was equal to the stupendous task.

When John Wilkes Booth fired the bullet that struck Abraham Lincoln down, immediately Lincoln's fame started for the stars and has grown steadily with the passing years. Today he stands unrivaled in the Valhalla of the American Republic, and who will doubt that one quality which has given him the pinnacle of fame was the brotherliness of the man, so natural, so simple and so sincere.

V

Thomas Curtis Clark, in his sonnet entitled "The Victim," with rare insight interprets the Apostle of Brotherhood and his apotheosis:

> Why was it this man of guileless heart
> Should bear the burden of the whole
>   world's guile?
> To him the smallest bird was
>   sacrosanct,
> And every child deserved of heaven's
>   smile;
> Yes cruel centuries of human hate
> Made him their victim—trapped by
>   time and fate;
> Nor did he quail, there was no other
>   man
> In all the earth whose soul could bear
>   the load;
> Nor was there any standing at his side
> Whose word could help, whose spirit
>   felt the goad
> Of destiny, the urge of Cosmic Right.
> He did not fail, this man of gentle
>   might;

He took the load, and facing tempests
   grim
Climbed Calvary—then night
   enveloped him.

In the convention of 1864 which renominated Lincoln, the chairman of the Illinois delegation stood up, and without coming forward, said this: "The people of the state of Illinois present to the people of the United States as candidate for the Presidency the name of Abraham Lincoln—God bless him!"

Today unnumbered millions rise to bless his name and to exclaim: "God bless the memory of Abraham Lincoln—Apostle of Brotherhood!"

15

On Wanting to Be "Let Alone"

I loathe my life; I would not live alway: *let me alone*; for my days are vanity.   JOB 7:16 (ASV)

How long wilt thou not look away from me, nor *let me alone* till I swallow down my spittle?   JOB 7:19 (ASV)

Are not my days few? cease then, and *let me alone*, that I may take comfort a little.   JOB 10:20 (ASV)

Hold your peace, *let me alone*, that I may speak; and let come on me what will.   JOB 13:13 (ASV)

FOUR times in the Book of Job occurs the exclamation "Let me alone." Each time it was the afflicted patriarch who spoke the bitter words. There was a reason. If ever a human being was a victim of crushing adversity, Job was that man. After the manner of lightning in a cloudless sky, stroke after stroke fell on this upright person. He was stripped of his possessions, his family all but wiped out, his health wrecked, and a loathsome disease made him an object not only of pity but also one of revulsion.

The scene pictured in this book of sublime drama is vivid and starkly realistic. Job is depicted sitting on an ash heap, scraping himself with a piece of crockery, and dreadfully low in mind and spirit. Why had this happened to him of all persons? Where was God, the just and the merciful? And was this the reward of fidelity, charity and integrity? Thus Job wondered, speculated and grieved. He even went so far as to curse the day of his birth.

To this miserable shadow of his one-time greatness and opulence there journey three friends who had heard that calamity had visited the good and venerated patriarch. Their names are familiar to all students of the Bible: Eliphaz the Temanite, Bildad the Shuhite, and Zophar the Naamathite—a precious trio. As they drew near and perceived the condition of their friend, they lifted up their voices and wept; and after the fashion of mourning in the Far East, rent their robes and sprinkled dust upon their heads. And because they saw that Job's grief was very great, they sat down with him on the ground, but withheld their speech for seven days and nights.

Job was the first to speak, and his three friends listened critically, for what he said was caustic and rebellious. Whereupon the so-called "comforters" gave Job a piece of their minds. They intimated that he was presumptuous in questioning the wisdom of the Almighty and flatly charged that the cause of his pitiful state was some grievous sin which he had committed. Job answered that, while he was not a perfect man, he had done no wrong that warranted the awful calamity which had befallen him.

Later, a fourth "comforter" joined in the conversation: a younger man, by name Elihu, the Buzite. He rates higher than Eliphaz, Bildad, and Zophar, being more intelligent and less pontifical. Elihu took higher ground when he intimated that there might be a remedial aspect to Job's suffering and some good salvaged from it. Yet Elihu also chided Job for his self-righteousness and bade him be humble and confess his sins.

I

"Let me alone!" This outburst of Job, four times recorded, is lustily human and therefore readily understood. In similar circumstances, and with far less provocation, we moderns repeat Job's pathetic plaint "Let me alone." For various reasons we do not wish to be disturbed, annoyed or put on the spot. We resent intrusions on our privacy, are suspicious of self-appointed advisors, preferring to be left to our own inclinations and devices. Nevertheless, "Let me alone" is a counsel of imperfection and the mood it connotes is not good for human beings, who were not made to be alone. Smarting under the smug assumptions of his censorious friends, sore stricken in mind and body, the bedeviled patriarch cried, irritably, "Let me alone!"

Grief may be, and frequently is, a selfish indulgence. It is possible to nurse our sorrows so as to keep them acute and to such an extent as to make ourselves, and those about us, miserable. Some years ago there was a popular song heard frequently over the air entitled "I'll Never Smile Again." The story is that a young widow wrote it while still mourning for her husband and declaring, "I'll never smile again until I smile with you." The melody of the song is plaintively beautiful, but the sentiment is unwholesome. To resolve never to smile again because of the loss of husband, wife, child, friend, is to let selfishness have its disabling way with us. No matter how bitter the experience, or how hard the going, we *must* smile again, for our own good and for the good of our kinspeople and our friends. In the wistful words of the Hoosier poet, Riley:

> Bring unto the sorrowing
> All release from pain,
> Let the lips of laughter
> Overflow again.

Job's "comforters" were brutally frank and totally lacking in tact. Not only so, but they were "preachy." Now, there is a time to preach, but not the kind of preaching the "comforters" inflicted upon this broken and pain-stricken patriarch of the land of Uz. They brought him logic and censure when what he yearned for was love and compassion.

Over against this ancient scene let me place a modern instance. Those familiar with the great names in English history, names that were on many lips in the middle of the past century, will recall Richard Cobden and John Bright. Cobden was an economist and a reformer of the unjust social order; Bright, one of the most famous orators of his day, of Quaker lineage, a humanitarian, statesman and prophet of righteousness. In 1841

Bright's beautiful young wife died, leaving him crushed utterly and wondering how he could ever take up the broken threads of his life again. Three days after her death Cobden called to see him, spoke some words of condolence, and then the two sat in silence for some time. Then Cobden looked up and said, "There are thousands of homes in England at this moment where wives, mothers, and children are dying of hunger. Now, when the first paroxysm of your grief is past, I would advise you to come with me, and we will never rest till the Corn Laws are repealed." "I accepted his invitation," Bright said in recounting the incident, "and from that time we never ceased to labor hard on behalf of the resolution which we had made." Thus did John Bright sublimate his grief.

The thing to note in this incident is the exquisite tact of Richard Cobden, come to comfort his sorrowing friend. No grief-stricken person could possibly wish to be let alone by one so understanding and so constructive in his advice. Compared with this comforter, Job's were like bulls in a china store. Instead of comforting him they needled him.

II

Not only did Job want to be let alone in his grief, but also in his ignorance. He sat in darkness yet he resented his friends' attempt to let light in. True, they were bungling in their approach, but they meant well. They wanted to tell him what they were sure he ought to hear, but Job didn't want to listen.

Pity the plight of those who see no cause for expanding their knowledge or conquering their prejudices. Usually they reason thus: "I am satisfied with the views I have inherited from my forebears. What was good enough for them is good enough for me. What they liked, I like. What they hated, I hate." Now if it were possible to inherit nothing but good from those who went before us, this position could be justified. Alas! we know better. Even in the case of those whose heritage is of high standards, noble thinking and superior gifts, it is still true that:

New occasions teach new duties,
    time makes ancient good uncouth;
They must upward still and onward,
    who would keep abreast of truth.

As the eloquent and brilliant Wendell Phillips once said, "To be as good as our fathers, we have to be better. To see as far as they saw we have to see further. . . . Be not like the figure on a coin, ever looking backward."

There is a term in law known as "mortmain," meaning "dead hand." Primarily the term had bearing in ecclesiastical courts, but in a secondary sense signifies the dead hand of the past that rests heavily upon society to its hurt. It may take the form of tradition, precedent or simply blind surrender to ideas, attitudes and methods made precious by inheritance. My long-time friend, the late Burris Jenkins of Kansas City, used to tell of a case which is relevant here. I think it had Kentucky for its source, but it might have been any of the other forty-seven states, Michigan, for instance. A gentleman motoring leisurely through an agricultural region observed a strangely shaped mound in a field and, being a man of scientific interests, his curiosity was aroused as to the nature of the formation. He stopped at the farmhouse, inquired for the proprietor of the place, and the two of them walked over to the mound, where the stranger examined its surface with no small enthusiasm. "My dear sir," he said to the farmer, "I may be mistaken, but I believe this is a relic of the Mound Builders. Have you ever thought of excavating to find out for yourself what is under this pile of earth?" The farmer, who was middle-aged, showed no interest whatsoever, and settled the question then and there: "This farm has been in our family for four generations. My grandfather never dug in that mound, neither did his father, and my father never explored it, and you can bet your last dollar I'll never dig it up." In short, "Let me alone!"

In this case it was a farmer who wanted to be let alone in his determination to conserve things as they were. But it could just as well have been a lawyer, a doctor, a clergyman, a business-man, a politician. The let-me-aloners are not limited to any one class, creed, or condition. They are everywhere in evidence. The proverb that "You can't teach an old dog new tricks," needs scrutiny as do most proverbial sayings. The usual explanation is that the old dog knows a lot of tricks and doesn't want to learn any new ones. I am not so sure of this interpretation. I suspect that you *can* teach an old dog new tricks if there is anybody around willing to take the time and patience to teach the dog how to execute some brand new didoes. Dogs seldom want to be let alone!

Over in Illinois, when Abraham Lincoln was a member of the state legislature, a charter for the establishment of Illinois College was up for consideration. Lincoln voted "Aye," but a fellow legislator voted "No," and followed it by saying: "I was born in a briar patch, rocked in a hog trough, and have never had my genius cramped by the pestilent air of a college." It is as clear as a sunbeam that this politician wished to be let utterly alone in his ignorance. There is a Biblical proverb which applies to all who are satisfied with their knowledge, be it much or little: "Seest thou a man wise in his own conceit? there is more hope of a fool than of him."

Job had his high moments, as, for instance, in replying to a harangue from Bildad, he made this lovely speech: "If I have withheld the poor from their desire, or have caused the eyes of the widow to fail, or have eaten my morsel alone . . . then let mine arm fall from my shoulder and mine arm be broken from the bone." There was a rainbow around Job's shoulder when he said that. Surely in the days of his prosperity he did not wish to be let alone.

III

This counsel of imperfection is not limited to individuals; it also infects nations, churches, institutions and organizations of every description. Today there is no nation big enough and strong enough to live to itself. Nationalism, called by an English churchman "the parasite on the body of the State," dies hard. There are still sincere and honest citizens who say, "The people of this country must keep America for Americans. We are isolationists and proud of it." Whatever this attitude may have meant fifty years ago, it means folly now. There is much to be said for co-operative wisdom, corporate endeavor and collective security among and with the free nations of the world, confronting, as they do, the terrifying menace of communism.

As for congregations bearing the Christian name that want to be let alone in their pride and selfishness, the case is all the more lamentable. Believing they have need of nothing, their self-deception is pitiful. "Look at our stately Gothic edifices," they boast, "our big-name preachers, our famous choirs and capacity audiences." Such congregations resemble the parrot that spent her days preening her feathers and prattling over and over again the words, "Pretty Poll, Pretty Poll." The ancient church at Laodicea wanted to be let alone in its complacency, its riches and vainglory. But God did not let that sinful church alone. He sent a messenger, who denounced the church as "poor, blind, and naked"—words that stung like the lash of a whip! A modern messenger of the Lord, the late Bishop James E. Freeman, coined an epigram that deserves to live, namely, "An insular church is an insolent church."

No, the Lord did not let Sodom and Gomorrah alone, or Nineveh, or Jerusalem, or Babylon. The Bible is a record of one long, never-ending drive against evil; disturbing, vexing, shocking, convicting nations, institutions and peoples of their wrongdoing and converting them. Moses didn't let his fellow Israelites alone in Egyptian slavery. Nathan the prophet didn't let David alone in his great sin but met him face to face, saying, "Thou art the man." Jesus didn't let Zaccheus alone, or Simon Peter, or Mary Magdalene, or a host of others. Paul didn't let Governor Felix alone in his adultery or King Herod Agrippa in his wickedness.

God didn't let Job alone in his piety, benevolences, affluence or adversity. Nor did the Lord let Job's "comforters" alone. He is represented in the drama as provoked with Eliphaz, Bildad and Zophar because of their folly in not speaking "of me the thing that is right, as my servant Job hath." In the end the Lord dispensed with emissaries and dealt with Job face to face, speaking to him from out of a whirlwind and saying, "Gird up now thy loins like a man; for I will demand of thee, and answer thou me."

Job answered, and the quintessence of his answer is in these words of humble contrition: "I have heard of thee by the hearing of the ear; but now mine eye seeth thee: wherefore I abhor myself and repent in dust and ashes."

For this splendid and moving drama of Job we should be profoundly grateful. Whoever wrote it was a genius, a poet and a theologian. According to the Book of Job, there is a mystery in suffering which the Lord has not seen fit to disclose. It is enough to know that He knows our frame, and the way we take, and that the Judge of all the earth is just.

Job wanted to be let alone, or thought he did. Unhappy as he was because his friends came to see him and gave him a piece of their minds, the likelihood is that he would have been unhappier had they not come. We do not live long until we learn that life simply will not let us alone; our relatives won't let us alone; the Church won't let us alone; the school won't let us alone; the law won't let us alone; business won't let us alone; our vocations won't let us alone; Government won't let us alone. Neither will the Living God let us alone!

That God will not let us alone is not a disturbing gospel, but one full of comfort. To be let severely alone by the Eternal God would be an abyss of loneliness and despair. If it is a fearful thing to fall *into* the hands of the Living God, it is a more terrible thing to fall *out* of His hands.

Even in the throes of the certain wages our sins must pay,

God seeks to save us to Himself and to the abundant life of the Spirit. "Billy" Sunday, in a vivid account of his conversion, used to say, "I staggered drunk into the arms of Jesus." Francis Thompson put it more poetically but no less vividly when he described the divine pursuit as the Hound of Heaven who, "with unhurrying chase and unperturbed pace," is ever on our trail, unwilling that one of us, even the least, should perish.

Let us hear then, the conclusion of the whole matter, concerning which much has been said: Not now, or ever, the petulant cry: "Let me alone," but, rather, the fervent prayer:

> O God, take us, break us, make us, and use us
> for Thyself and Thy children, now, and forevermore!

Date Due